AT A GLANCE

Essential Court Tables for Ancillary Relief

THE FAMILY LAW
BAR ASSOCIATION

FLBA

Copyright © The Family Law Bar Association 1995
All rights reserved

First edition published 1992, reprinted 1992
Second edition published 1993
Third edition published 1994
Fourth edition published 1995

A CIP catalogue record for this book is available from the
British Library

ISBN 1 872362 55 9

**Further copies of this book and future editions
may be ordered from**

**The Publications Secretary
The Family Law Bar Association
Queen Elizabeth Building
Temple
London EC4Y 9BS**

**Telephone 0171 797 7837
Fax 0171 353 5422
DX Number: LDE 339**

Produced for The FLBA by
Class Publishing
7 Melrose Terrace
London W6 7RL

Cover design by Wendy Bann
Edited by Susan Bosanko

Printed by
Cheney & Sons Ltd
Beaumont Road
Banbury
Oxon OX16 7RH

Contents

Reflections on Duxbury

The time has now come to take a look at the bounds beyond which it is unhelpful to develop the sophistication of **Duxbury** calculations. The purpose of these Reflections is to stimulate (and perhaps even to guide) debate about whether the underlying methodology should be further elaborated, or the courts should now call a halt.

What remains fundamental to such a discussion is that these calculations are at best only a guide for use by practitioners and the court. They must be regarded as an adjunct to rather than as a substitute for the discretionary exercise which section 25 imposes on the judge: see the citations at page 20.

There is thus but limited utility in refinement beyond a certain point, with the risk that it may invest the result with a spurious illusion of authenticity. It is to avoid that semblance that the results in Table 19 are rounded to the nearest £1,000. What ever else the future may hold, the one thing which can be predicted with absolute certainty is that the recipient of a **Duxbury** award will invest and spend it in a way the program did not envisage, and is unlikely to die on the date appointed by the life tables as the fund finally sinks exhausted away.

A consistency of approach and a shared raft of assumptions should therefore be developed amongst those practitioners (including accountants and actuaries) to whose expertise the parties resort. The issues over which it would be possible for experts reasonably to disagree should not have forensic time devoted to them if the outcome, however interesting, does not affect the result. Such a self-limiting ordinance, if it could be applied and honoured, would be entirely consistent with the principles enshrined in the Practice Direction dated 31 January 1995, aimed at minimising cost and delay in family proceedings. Hence, issues the subject of expert evidence are to be reduced or eliminated wherever possible.

The assumptions which underpin our **Duxbury** centrespread are set out in the text below Table 19. Of these the real rate of return provides most potent scope for dissension. In previous editions 5% and then 4.5% were adopted as appropriate, but this year the results reflect the selection of 4.25% as (it is to be hoped) a definitive rate. This is the rate adopted in recent but (as we go to press) yet unreported decisions in two Divisions of the High Court: **F v F**, Fam Div, 24 October 1994, an ancillary relief claim heard by Thorpe J; and **Nott v Ward**, Ch Div, 13 December 1994, an Inheritance Act case determined by HHJ Bromley QC.

Reflections on Duxbury

Practice in the Queen's Bench Division may come under review in the wake of the recently-published Law Commission report *Structured Settlements and Interim and Provisional Damages* (Law Com. No. 224, 1994) and the second edition of *Actuarial Tables for use in Personal Injury and Fatal Accident Cases* (HMSO, 1994). Each recommends the adoption of scientifically selected multipliers. This would make the approach to capitalisation of damages for loss of income and future annual costs consistent with **Duxbury** principles.

In the introductory material to *Actuarial Tables* the Ogden Committee point out that for a payee to be certain to receive an inflation-proof income for the period to which the loss relates it would be necessary to invest in Index-Linked Government Stock. The return upon these has historically ranged between 2.5% and 4.5% gross. The rate applicable on 30 January 1995 was 3.89% before tax (source: *Financial Times*). By contrast the gross real return on equities has over the 25 years to 1993 averaged 5.8% (source: The BZW Equity-Gilt Study *Investment in the London Stock Market since 1918*).

After tax these rates of return would be still lower, to an extent dependent on the recipient's individual circumstances. But it must be borne in mind that allowance in the **Duxbury** figures is made for all bands of tax at prevailing rates, uplifted annually for assumed future inflation. The lower the percentage real rate of return selected, the higher the capital fund required. So the choice made for these **Duxbury** tables of 4.25% should be regarded as fair to each spouse, and designed to cover such considerations as any professional expense in managing the award, once made.

Whereas therefore the previous editions of *At A Glance* have suggested that it was a matter for evidence and argument in each case what assumptions should be adopted, it may now be that such a laissez-faire approach is outmoded. It would be better to accept that (for the illustrative purpose which is all that the calculation can provide) an industry-standard of 4.25% should be adopted as the real rate of return in current and foreseeable financial circumstances.

Acknowledgements

The Family Law Bar Association acknowledges with thanks the assistance it has received from the following who have agreed to material derived from them being incorporated in this volume:

The Automobile Association
The Bank of England
The Central Statistical Office
Coopers & Lybrand
Economist Intelligence Unit
The Equitable Life
Ernst & Young
Family Law

The Financial Times Business Centre
The Halifax Building Society
Her Majesty's Stationery Office
The Independent Schools Information Service
The National Foster Care Association
Peter Lobbenberg & Co
Savings Certificate and SAYE Office

Particular thanks are due to Martha Street for considerable assistance with Tables 23 and 24.

The Family Law Bar Association thanks the Editorial Committee responsible for the production of this volume:

The Hon. Mr Justice Singer
James Holman QC
Paul Coleridge QC
Valentine Le Grice
Nicholas Mostyn
Gavin Smith
Katharine Davidson
Timothy Bishop

Although care has been taken to ensure the reliability of the contents of this volume neither The Family Law Bar Association nor any of its officers or members warrants their accuracy.

The Family Law Bar Association publishes *At a Glance* annually, incorporating fresh and up-dated material. The Editorial Committee would welcome suggestions, whether for the improvement of existing or for the addition of further tables.

Tables 6, 11 (part), 19, 22, 26, 27, 28 and Tax Relief on Maintenance are the copyright of Nicholas Mostyn; Leading Cases is the copyright of Nicholas Mostyn and Gavin Smith. They have asserted their rights in accordance with the Copyright, Designs and Patents Act 1988, and the material may not be reproduced without their permission.

The Perpetual Calendar is taken from the *Collins Management Diary,* published by the Stationery and Diary Division of HarperCollins Publishers and is reproduced with their permission.

Table 1   Retail Price Index

	1956	1957	1958	1959	1960	1961	1962	1963	1964	1965
Jan	11.25	11.74	12.17	12.42	12.37	12.62	13.21	13.56	13.84	14.47
Feb	11.25	11.74	12.09	12.40	12.37	12.62	13.23	13.69	13.84	14.47
Mar	11.38	11.71	12.19	12.40	12.34	12.67	13.28	13.71	13.89	14.52
Apr	11.56	11.76	12.32	12.32	12.40	12.75	13.46	13.74	14.02	14.80
May	11.53	11.76	12.29	12.27	12.40	12.78	13.51	13.74	14.14	14.85
Jun	11.51	11.89	12.40	12.29	12.47	12.90	13.59	13.74	14.20	14.90
Jul	11.48	11.99	12.19	12.40	12.50	12.90	13.54	13.66	14.20	14.90
Aug	11.51	11.96	12.19	12.29	12.42	13.00	13.43	13.61	14.25	14.93
Sep	11.48	11.94	12.19	12.22	12.42	13.00	13.41	13.66	14.25	14.93
Oct	11.56	12.04	12.29	12.29	12.52	13.00	13.41	13.71	14.27	14.96
Nov	11.58	12.12	12.34	12.37	12.60	13.16	13.46	13.74	14.37	15.01
Dec	11.63	12.17	12.40	12.40	12.62	13.18	13.51	13.76	14.42	15.08

	1966	1967	1968	1969	1970	1971	1972	1973	1974	1975
Jan	15.11	15.67	16.07	17.06	17.90	19.42	21.01	22.64	25.35	30.39
Feb	15.11	15.67	16.15	17.16	18.00	19.54	21.12	22.79	25.78	30.90
Mar	15.13	15.67	16.20	17.21	18.10	19.70	21.19	22.92	26.00	31.51
Apr	15.34	15.79	16.50	17.41	18.38	20.13	21.39	23.35	26.89	32.72
May	15.44	15.79	16.50	17.39	18.43	20.25	21.50	23.52	27.28	34.09
Jun	15.49	15.84	16.58	17.47	18.48	20.38	21.62	23.65	27.55	34.75
Jul	15.41	15.74	16.58	17.47	18.63	20.51	21.70	23.75	27.81	35.11
Aug	15.51	15.72	16.60	17.41	18.61	20.53	21.88	23.83	27.83	35.31
Sep	15.49	15.69	16.63	17.47	18.71	20.56	22.00	24.03	28.14	35.61
Oct	15.51	15.82	16.70	17.59	18.91	20.66	22.31	24.51	28.69	36.12
Nov	15.61	15.92	16.76	17.64	19.04	20.79	22.38	24.69	29.20	36.55
Dec	15.64	16.02	16.96	17.77	19.16	20.89	22.48	24.87	29.63	37.01

	1976	1977	1978	1979	1980	1981	1982	1983	1984	1985
Jan	37.49	43.70	48.03	52.52	62.18	70.29	78.73	82.61	86.84	91.20
Feb	37.97	44.13	48.31	52.95	63.07	70.93	78.76	82.97	87.20	91.94
Mar	38.17	44.56	48.62	53.38	63.93	71.99	79.44	83.12	87.48	92.80
Apr	38.91	45.70	49.33	54.30	66.11	74.07	81.04	84.28	88.64	94.78
May	39.34	46.06	49.61	54.73	66.72	74.55	81.62	84.64	88.97	95.21
Jun	39.54	46.54	49.99	55.67	67.35	74.98	81.85	84.84	89.20	95.41
Jul	39.62	46.59	50.22	58.07	67.91	75.31	81.88	85.30	89.10	95.23
Aug	40.18	46.82	50.54	58.53	68.06	75.87	81.90	85.68	89.94	95.49
Sep	40.71	47.07	50.75	59.11	68.49	76.30	81.85	86.06	90.11	95.44
Oct	41.44	47.28	50.98	59.72	68.92	76.98	82.26	86.36	90.67	95.59
Nov	42.03	47.50	51.33	60.25	69.48	77.79	82.66	86.67	90.95	95.92
Dec	42.59	47.76	51.76	60.68	69.86	78.28	82.51	86.89	90.87	96.05

	1986	1987	1988	1989	1990	1991	1992	1993	1994	1995
Jan	96.25	100.0	103.3	111.0	119.5	130.2	135.6	137.9	141.3	146.0
Feb	96.60	100.4	103.7	111.8	120.2	130.9	136.3	138.8	142.1	
Mar	96.73	100.6	104.1	112.3	121.4	131.4	136.7	139.3	142.5	
Apr	97.67	101.8	105.8	114.3	125.1	133.1	138.8	140.6	144.2	
May	97.85	101.9	106.2	115.0	126.2	133.5	139.3	141.1	144.7	
Jun	97.79	101.9	106.6	115.4	126.7	134.1	139.3	141.1	144.7	
Jul	97.52	101.8	106.7	115.5	126.8	133.8	138.8	140.7	144.0	
Aug	97.82	102.1	107.9	115.8	128.1	134.1	138.9	141.3	144.7	
Sep	98.30	102.4	108.4	116.6	129.3	134.6	139.4	141.9	145.0	
Oct	98.45	102.9	109.5	117.5	130.3	135.1	139.9	141.8	145.2	
Nov	99.29	103.4	110.0	118.5	130.0	135.6	139.7	141.6	145.3	
Dec	99.62	103.3	110.3	118.8	129.9	135.7	139.2	141.9	146.0	

Figures before January 1987 have been rebased. Those from January 1987 are official Central Statistical Office (CSO) figures, published to one decimal place only. The latest RPI figures can be obtained by polling the CSO Statfax service on 0336 416037 (premium rate); by telephoning its recorded message service on 0171 217 4905; or from its Public Enquiry Service on 0171 270 6363 or 6364. More detailed information may be obtained from the *Employment Gazette* tables 6.1-6.8 or the CSO *Monthly Digest of Statistics* tables 18.1-18.3.

How to calculate the effect of inflation
from one month to any subsequent month

The formula is $X \times A \div B$

Where **X** is the figure to be inflated
A is the RPI for the later month
B is the RPI for the earlier month
(e.g. when asset acquired or previous order made)

Table 2   Financial Times Index

Level of the FT All-Share Index at month-end

Year	Jan	Feb	Mar	Apr	May	Jun	Jul	Aug	Sep	Oct	Nov	Dec
83	395.02	399.35	411.94	439.29	437.63	458.91	445.91	450.36	445.53	437.38	461.87	470.50
84	501.36	493.12	542.20	534.83	477.21	487.74	474.83	520.47	535.86	543.48	560.26	592.94
85	614.62	508.28	616.26	622.11	634.16	595.54	603.46	646.26	626.24	670.64	696.53	682.94
86	696.41	750.83	810.48	816.40	788.92	815.70	771.80	817.06	768.79	807.27	815.34	835.48
87	903.29	983.12	1,000.04	1,023.58	1,097.29	1,153.12	1,202.19	1,146.69	1,208.89	887.33	796.31	870.22
88	915.84	908.08	896.75	928.19	923.52	963.01	965.18	911.17	946.27	965.54	933.45	926.59
89	1,054.97	1,042.60	1,076.15	1,090.04	1,091.06	1,101.67	1,173.25	1,207.45	1,169.55	1,080.79	1,138.67	1,204.70
90	1,167.15	1,122.26	1,114.94	1,043.16	1,154.24	1,171.28	1,147.05	1,051.08	962.18	992.67	1,032.11	1,032.25
91	1,036.24	1,150.01	1,193.33	1,202.75	1,201.85	1,161.19	1,235.89	1,268.62	1,265.96	1,238.63	1,168.95	1,187.70
92	1,227.63	1,229.84	1,171.71	1,282.75	1,311.79	1,216.62	1,143.14	1,096.99	1,206.16	1,256.67	1,313.02	1,363.79
93	1,364.33	1,396.53	1,408.07	1,388.88	1,403.42	1,432.31	1,448.76	1,537.21	1,506.55	1,565.37	1,556.45	1,682.17
94	1,745.97	1,675.49	1,561.97	1,580.44	1,501.22	1,463.35	1,545.74	1,626.64	1,510.97	1,536.31	1,528.12	1,521.44
95	1,480.56											

Table 3   Judgment Debt Interest Rates

Pursuant to s 17 Judgments Act 1838

	Date	%
Before	20 April 1971	4.00
Since	20 April 1971	7.50
	1 March 1977	10.00
	3 December 1979	12.50
	9 June 1980	15.00
	8 June 1982	14.00
	10 November 1982	12.00
	16 April 1985	15.00
	1 April 1993	8.00

As well as applying to High Court judgments generally, from 1 July 1991 County Court judgment debts over £5,000 have attracted interest at the rates shown above.

Table 4   Interest Base Rates

This table shows the dates of change in the base rate of the four largest London Clearing Banks (Barclays, Lloyds, Midland and National Westminster) at close of business on the respective days

Date	New rate (%)	Date	New rate (%)	Date	New rate (%)
1980		**1985**		8 August	10.75*
4 July	16.00	11 January	10.50	9 August	11.00
25 November	14.00	14 January	12.00	25 August	11.50*
		28 January	14.00	26 August	12.00
1981		20 March	13.75*	25 November	13.00
11 March	12.00	21 March	13.50		
16 September	14.00	29 March	13.25*	**1989**	
1 October	16.00	2 April	13.125*	24 May	14.00
14 October	15.50	12 April	12.875*	5 October	15.00
9 November	15.00	19 April	12.675*		
3 December	14.50	12 June	12.50	**1990**	
		7 July	12.25*	8 October	14.00
1982		16 July	12.00		
12 January	14.00	29 July	11.75*	**1991**	
25 February	13.50	30 July	11.50	13 February	13.50
12 March	13.00			27 February	13.00
8 June	12.50	**1986**		25 March	12.50
13 July	12.00	9 January	12.50	12 April	12.00
2 August	11.50	19 March	11.50	24 May	11.50
18 August	11.00	8 April	11.25*	12 July	11.00
31 August	10.50	9 April	11.00	4 September	10.50
7 October	10.00	24 April	10.50		
14 October	9.50	27 May	10.00	**1992**	
4 November	9.00	14 October	11.00	5 May	10.00
26 November	10.125*			16 September	12.00
		1987		17 September	10.00
1983		10 March	10.50	22 September	9.00
12 January	11.00	19 March	10.00	16 October	8.00
15 March	10.50	29 April	9.50	13 November	7.00
15 April	10.00	11 May	9.00		
15 June	9.50	7 August	10.00	**1993**	
4 October	9.00	26 October	9.50	26 January	6.00
		5 November	9.00	23 November	5.50
1984		4 December	8.50		
7 March	8.875*			**1994**	
15 March	8.625*	**1988**		8 February	5.25
10 May	9.125*	2 February	9.00	12 September	5.75
27 June	9.25	17 March	8.50	7 December	6.25
9 July	10.00	11 April	8.00		
11 July	11.00*	18 May	7.50	**1995**	
12 July	12.00	3 June	8.00	2 February	6.75
9 August	11.50	6 June	8.25*		
10 August	11.00	7 June	8.50		
20 August	10.50	22 June	9.00		
7 November	10.00	29 June	9.50		
20 November	9.875*	5 July	10.00		
23 November	9.625*	19 July	10.50		

An asterisk denotes that for that period, there was a spread not exceeding ± 0.5%.

Table 5   National Savings

March 1995 value of £100 of Index-linked National Savings purchased in any month since June 1975

	Jan	Feb	Mar	Apr	May	Jun	Jul	Aug	Sep	Oct	Nov	Dec
75						559.75	537.68	527.70	522.49	519.53	514.84	507.75
76	501.87	495.79	489.57	483.46	480.95	472.00	466.93	464.16	463.33	457.01	451.12	443.27
77	437.20	431.55	420.76	416.69	412.77	402.55	399.53	395.20	394.78	392.89	390.60	388.86
78	387.03	385.03	382.82	380.66	378.30	372.85	370.77	367.79	366.16	363.77	362.32	360.66
79	358.21	355.22	350.15	347.34	344.52	338.71	336.09	330.54	317.09	314.66	311.59	308.40
80	305.71	303.58	296.37	292.29	288.37	278.88	276.36	273.78	271.57	270.94	269.19	267.48
81	265.43	264.03	262.41	260.10	256.35	249.24	247.67	246.17	245.13	243.35	242.02	239.91
82	237.41	236.00	234.66	234.59	232.60	228.04	226.43	225.88	225.82	225.76	225.48	223.94
83	222.51	222.50	221.90	220.55	219.74	216.33	215.05	214.20	212.70	211.39	210.06	209.01
84	207.95	207.00	206.78	205.57	204.52	201.48	200.38	199.58	199.43	197.21	196.42	194.82
85	193.84	193.52	192.40	184.43	182.30	178.08	184.17	183.77	184.07	183.55	183.61	183.25
86	182.71	182.48	182.10	180.58	180.34	178.63	178.31	182.48	182.99	182.47	181.62	181.32
87	179.82	179.24	178.59	177.03	176.68	174.60	174.42	174.45	174.65	174.15	173.67	172.83
88	172.03	172.24	172.32	170.81	170.16	167.48	166.89	166.27	166.12	164.29	163.55	161.99
89	161.27	160.82	159.85	157.94	157.25	154.55	153.61	153.09	152.99	152.58	151.57	150.43
90	149.19	148.79	147.91	146.41	144.36	139.56	126.54	125.86	125.56	124.09	122.77	121.64
91	121.70	121.59	121.11	115.85	115.31	113.76	113.33	112.75	112.90	112.55	112.04	111.55
92	111.04	110.86	110.86	108.64	108.28	106.62	106.19	106.15	106.49	106.36	105.94	108.71
93	108.61	108.75	109.51	108.64	108.08	106.92	106.37	106.27	106.33	105.71	105.09	104.99
94	104.66	104.29	104.58									

Notes

The table gives the March 1995 value of a £100 Index-linked Certificate purchased in each of the months shown. There is no increase in value within the first year for which an Index-linked Certificate is held. All returns are tax-free. The index-linked increase is based on the January 1995 Retail Price Index figure of 146.0, an increase of 3.3% over the previous year.

Retirement Issue & 2nd Issue

The value shown includes the index-linked increase (earned on the first of the month) and all supplements. It also includes 4% bonuses earned on the fifth and tenth anniversary of purchase. These Certificates now earn index-linking only, unless the tenth anniversary bonus is still due (final bonus payable on 29 June 1995).

3rd, 4th, 5th, 6th & 7th Issues

The value shown includes the index-linked increase and any Extra Interest (both earned on the day of the month on which the certificates were purchased).

The 3rd and 4th Index-linked Issues earn index-linking monthly after the fifth anniversary of purchase, plus 0.5% on each following anniversary.
5th Issue issued 1 November 1992 to 12 November 1992: value £105.94 as shown *above*.
6th Issue issued 13 November 1992 to 30 November 1992: value £109.34.
6th Issue issued 1 December 1993 to 16 December 1993: value £104.99 as shown *above*.
7th Issue issued 17 December 1993 to 31 December 1993: value £104.67.

Non-index-linked National Savings

The 7th to 35th Issues earn interest following maturity at a variable tax-exempt General Extension Rate (3.51% as at January 1995); valuation can be obtained by telephoning 0191 374 5022 or by writing to National Savings, Millburngate House, Durham DH99 1NS.

Table 6 Inflation and Savings

This table illustrates the diminishing value of a £10,000 building society or bank deposit, and of the gross annual income it produces

Years since investment	A Real value of deposit	B Real value of income	C Real value of deposit	D Real value of income
0	10,000	700	10,000	1,100
1	9,804	686	9,434	1,038
2	9,612	673	8,900	979
3	9,423	660	8,396	924
4	9,238	647	7,921	871
5	9,057	634	7,473	822
6	8,880	622	7,050	775
7	8,706	609	6,651	732
8	8,535	597	6,274	690
9	8,368	586	5,919	651
10	8,203	574	5,584	614
11	8,043	563	5,268	579
12	7,885	552	4,970	547
13	7,730	541	4,688	516
14	7,579	531	4,423	487
15	7,430	520	4,173	459
16	7,284	510	3,936	433
17	7,142	500	3,714	409
18	7,002	490	3,503	385
19	6,864	481	3,305	364
20	6,730	471	3,118	343
21	6,598	462	2,942	324
22	6,468	453	2,775	305
23	6,342	444	2,618	288
24	6,217	435	2,470	272
25	6,095	427	2,330	256

The assumptions

Columns **A** & **B** give the results on the assumption of 2% inflation and 7% gross interest.

Columns **C** & **D** give the results on the assumption of 6% inflation and 11% gross interest.

In neither case is interest reinvested nor account taken of tax.

While inflation is currently low, over the last decade it has averaged 6.07% p.a.

Table 7 Exchange Rates

Annual average exchange rates of 20 currencies for the past 10 years

	Australia dollar	Austria schilling	Belgium franc	Canada dollar	Denmark kroner
85	1.86	26.59	76.34	1.77	13.63
86	2.20	22.37	65.47	2.04	11.86
87	2.34	20.69	61.12	2.17	11.19
88	2.28	21.97	65.38	2.19	11.97
89	2.07	21.67	64.52	1.94	11.97
90	2.29	20.24	59.44	2.08	11.01
91	2.27	20.58	60.23	2.03	11.28
92	2.40	19.36	56.64	2.13	10.63
93	2.21	17.47	51.91	1.94	9.74
94	2.09	17.46	51.12	2.09	9.72

	Europe ecu	France franc	Germany mark	Greece drachma	Holland guilder
85	1.70	11.55	3.78	180	4.27
86	1.49	10.16	3.18	205	3.59
87	1.42	9.84	2.94	222	3.31
88	1.51	10.60	3.12	252	3.52
89	1.49	10.45	3.08	266	3.47
90	1.40	9.69	2.88	282	3.24
91	1.43	9.95	2.93	321	3.30
92	1.36	9.32	2.75	335	3.10
93	1.28	8.51	2.48	366	2.85
94	1.29	8.49	2.48	371	2.78

	Hong Kong dollar	Ireland punt	Italy lira	Japan yen	Norway kroner
85	10.11	1.22	2,463	307	11.07
86	11.45	1.09	2,186	247	10.84
87	12.78	1.10	2,123	237	11.02
88	13.89	1.17	2,315	228	11.59
89	12.78	1.16	2,247	226	11.30
90	13.91	1.08	2,133	257	11.14
91	13.74	1.10	2,187	238	11.44
92	13.67	1.04	2,163	224	10.93
93	11.51	1.05	2,514	164	11.06
94	11.85	1.02	2,467	156	10.79

	Portugal escudo	Spain peseta	Sweden kroner	Switzerland franc	USA dollar
85	221	220	11.09	3.16	1.30
86	219	205	10.44	2.64	1.47
87	231	202	10.38	2.44	1.64
88	256	207	10.90	2.60	1.78
89	258	194	10.56	2.68	1.64
90	254	181	10.54	2.47	1.79
91	255	183	10.67	2.53	1.77
92	238	180	10.23	2.48	1.77
93	260	191	11.70	2.22	1.50
94	254	205	11.80	2.09	1.53

Figures denote units of currency per pound sterling.

Table 8   International Living Costs

An index of comparative city living costs in January 1995

Index	City	Index	City	Index	City	Index	City
196	Tokyo	107	Frankfurt	92	New York	82	Lisbon
121	Geneva	107	Moscow	90*	Athens	79*	Rio de Janeiro
119	Paris	106	Brussels	90	Sydney	73	Abu Dhabi
116	Vienna	106	Hong Kong	88*	Beijing	63*	Istanbul
113	Copenhagen	103	Amsterdam	87	Madrid	53*	Prague
111*	Lagos	**100**	**London**	85	Rome	43	Bombay

Notes

Centred on London at 100, the index illustrates the cost of living in 23 other cities around the world.

The ratings are based on the survey published in December 1994 by the Economist Intelligence Unit (telephone 0171 830 1150), adjusted to February 1995 to reflect exchange rate movements. No such adjustment has been made for the asterisked cities where their relatively high inflation rate would produce a distorting effect.

Full reports for these and a further 97 cities are prepared every 6 months, based on the cost of a basket of over 170 goods and services including food, alcohol, tobacco, household supplies, utilities, domestic help, clothing, transport, recreation and entertainment.

It should be stressed that this index will fluctuate frequently as its underlying price data comparisons are sensitive to both exchange rates and inflation.

Table 9   Foster Care Allowances

NFCA recommended minimum fostering allowances for the year beginning 1 April 1995

Age of child (years)	National (£ per week)	London (£ per week)
0-4	55.33	64.91
5-10	68.60	80.51
11-15	85.41	100.19
16 +	110.59	129.81

Every year the National Foster Care Association (NFCA) recommends a minimum fostering allowance for the coming year, and publishes a full survey (*Foster Care Finance*) of the allowances paid by each local authority.

The NFCA recommended allowance varies according to the age of the child and whether or not the placement is in London.

Incorporated in the above allowances is a sum (equivalent to four extra weeks' payments) recommended by the NFCA to cover the cost of birthdays, holidays and religious festivals.

Foster Care Finance may be purchased from the NFCA, Leonard House, 5-7 Marshalsea Road, London SE1 1EP (telephone 0171 828 6266).

Table 10   Car Running Costs

Figures in the Cost per mile table *opposite* are calculated from the data *below*

Note: apart from the 1995-96 Car Benefit charges and Fuel charges *opposite*, these tables are compiled from information published by the AA in April 1994. An updated table incorporating the November 1994 Budget changes may be obtained from the AA from April 1995.

Standing charges: cost per annum (£)

	Engine capacity (cc)				
	up to 1,100	1,101 to 1,400	1,401 to 2,000	2,001 to 3,000	3,001 to 4,500
Car licence	130.00	130.00	130.00	130.00	130.00
Insurance	252.73	325.79	393.00	578.00	627.00
Depreciation	866.87	1,276.87	1,805.47	3,327.29	4,479.15
AA subscription	62.00	62.00	62.00	62.00	62.00
Totals	1,311.60	1,794.66	2,390.47	4,097.29	5,298.15

Standing charges: cost per mile (pence)

Annual mileage	Engine capacity (cc)				
	up to 1,100	1,101 to 1,400	1,401 to 2,000	2,001 to 3,000	3,001 to 4,500
5,000	26.24	35.90	47.80	81.94	105.96
10,000	13.12	17.95	23.90	40.97	52.98
15,000	9.90	13.67	18.34	31.75	41.29
20,000	9.16	12.80	17.37	30.47	39.93
25,000	8.71	12.29	16.78	29.70	39.10
30,000	7.26	10.24	13.99	24.75	32.59

Running costs: cost per mile (pence)

	Engine capacity (cc)				
	up to 1,100	1,101 to 1,400	1,401 to 2,000	2,001 to 3,000	3,001 to 4,500
Petrol	5.79	6.62	7.72	10.53	11.59
Oil	0.26	0.27	0.28	0.34	0.55
Tyres	0.66	0.86	1.05	2.01	2.59
Servicing	0.76	0.76	0.76	1.19	1.68
Repairs & replacements	2.80	3.18	3.26	5.00	5.14
Totals	10.27	11.69	13.07	19.07	21.55
For each 1p change in the cost per litre of petrol, add/subtract	0.11	0.13	0.15	0.21	0.23

Table 10 Car Running Costs

Total car running and maintenance costs according to engine capacity

Cost per mile (pence)

Annual mileage	Engine capacity (cc)				
	up to 1,100	1,101 to 1,400	1,401 to 2,000	2,001 to 3,000	3,001 to 4,500
5,000	36.51	47.59	60.87	101.01	127.51
10,000	23.39	29.64	36.97	60.04	74.53
15,000	20.17	25.36	31.41	50.82	62.84
20,000	19.43	24.49	30.44	49.54	61.48
25,000	18.98	23.98	29.85	48.77	60.65
30,000	17.53	21.93	27.06	43.82	54.14

The assumptions

Insurance is average cost of fully comprehensive policy with 60% no claims allowance.

Depreciation is based on average cost of a new car run for 10,000 miles per annum.

AA membership includes Relay service.

Petrol is unleaded petrol at 51.00p per litre.

Tyres have estimated life of 30,000 miles.

Servicing is routine servicing costs; older cars may have greater costs.

Repairs and renovations estimated for normal wear and tear (i.e. no major repairs).

Fuel charges 1995-96 (£)

Engine capacity (cc)	Petrol	Diesel
Up to 1,400	670	605
1,401 to 2,000	850	605
2,001 and over	1,260	780

Car Benefit charges 1995-96

Annual business mileage	Benefit*	Second car*
Up to 2,499	35%	35%
2,500 to 17,999	23⅓%	35%
18,000 and over	11⅔%	23⅓%

Fuel and Car Benefit charges each give rise to additional notional taxable income.

*Taxed as a percentage of list price on up to £80,000. Special rules over this limit and for 'classic' cars.

Cars at least 4 years old on 5 April 1996: charged at ⅔ of above rates.

Table 11   School Fees

Range of termly fees each year for various types of independent school

Year	Pre-prep (3-8)	Junior school (8-13)		Senior school (11-18)			
	Boys and girls	Boys and girls		Girls' schools		Boys' schools	
	Day	Day	Boarding	Day	Boarding	Day	Boarding
84	100-200	330-980	700-1,480	430-1,030	830-1,530	300-1,300	830-1,900
85	100-200	350-1,055	730-1,600	490-1,120	870-1,610	325-1,400	880-2,025
86	100-300	350-1,100	800-1,650	500-1,150	1,000-1,700	360-1,500	950-2,200
87	150-350	350-1,500	800-1,950	500-1,300	1,000-2,000	500-2,000	1,000-2,250
88	150-400	350-1,500	800-1,800	500-1,350	1,100-2,100	500-1,750	1,100-2,350
89	200-500	350-1,500	900-2,000	600-1,500	1,350-2,400	600-2,000	1,200-2,800
90	250-550	450-1,550	1,100-2,150	800-1,600	1,600-2,600	800-2,100	1,400-2,900
91	300-700	600-1,650	1,300-2,500	900-1,900	1,900-3,400	900-2,500	1,900-3,600
92	300-700	600-1,900	1,400-2,800	1,000-2,100	2,100-3,500	1,000-2,600	2,100-3,700
93	300-1,000	700-2,000	1,600-2,900	1,100-2,200	2,300-3,600	1,100-2,800	2,300-3,800
94	400-1,000	700-2,000	1,800-3,000	1,100-2,300	2,300-3,900	1,100-2,900	2,300-4,000

Rate of increase

Analysis of the rate of increase in school fees between 1984 and 1994 (Table A *below*) shows an average increase for all schools (excluding pre-prep) of **13.4% p.a.** Average annual inflation over the period was 6.1% p.a., so as a rule of thumb it is reasonable to project a **real rate of increase** in school fees of **7.3% p.a.** They will therefore cost the person paying the fees 7.3% more each year in real terms. ISIS (the Independent Schools Information Service) predict a 4%-5% increase in 1995.

An example showing the effect of this real rate of increase on a parent with an initial net income of £40,000 is given in Table B *below*.

Table B assumptions

Net income increases by 2% annually

School fees increase by 9.3% annually

Table A

Category	Average annual increase
Pre-prep	36.7%
Junior day school	10.6%
Junior boarding school	12.0%
Senior schools	
Girls' day schools	13.3%
Girls' boarding schools	16.3%
Boys' day schools	15.0%
Boys' boarding schools	13.1%

Table B

Year	Net income (£)	School fees (£)	% of income paid
1	40,000	5,000	12.5
2	40,800	5,465	13.4
3	41,616	5,973	14.4
4	42,448	6,529	15.4
5	43,297	7,136	16.5
6	44,163	7,800	17.7
7	45,046	8,525	18.9
8	45,947	9,318	20.3

Table 12   House Price Indices

Standardised indices showing change in property prices since 1987

UK indices (by property type)

Year	All houses			New houses			Existing houses		
	Index	%	Av'ge price	Index	%	Av'ge price	Index	%	Av'ge price
87	149.9	15.4	47,482	141.9	12.1	54,411	151.6	16.0	46,661
88	184.8	23.3	57,594	175.4	23.6	67,535	186.7	23.2	56,424
89	223.1	20.8	61,163	206.2	17.6	73,561	226.5	21.3	59,278
90	223.2	0.0	64,729	207.8	0.8	77,405	225.8	(0.3)	62,903
91	220.5	(1.2)	68,130	204.0	(1.8)	70,987	223.1	(1.2)	67,717
92	208.1	(5.6)	64,309	197.2	(5.8)	68,634	210.2	(5.8)	63,797
93	202.1	(2.9)	62,455	195.0	(1.1)	67,856	204.0	(3.0)	61,911
94	203.1	0.5	62,750	195.5	0.3	68,032	205.1	0.5	62,250

Regional indices (all houses)

Year	North		Yorks/Humb.		N. West		E. Midlands		W. Midlands		E. Anglia	
	Index	%	Index	%	Index	%	Index	%	Index	%	Index	%
87	122.0	6.5	130.5	9.1	127.9	7.6	145.2	14.6	136.9	14.6	174.1	25.3
88	136.7	12.1	155.0	18.8	149.0	16.5	187.3	28.8	185.8	35.7	248.9	43.0
89	182.8	33.7	222.7	43.6	202.0	35.5	243.2	30.0	240.7	29.6	255.5	2.6
90	207.7	13.6	237.5	6.6	227.4	12.6	234.4	(3.6)	238.0	(1.1)	225.8	(11.6)
91	213.5	2.8	240.4	1.2	236.3	3.9	227.9	(2.8)	240.4	1.0	214.4	(5.0)
92	210.1	(1.6)	231.9	(3.6)	226.1	(4.3)	214.4	(5.9)	229.4	(4.6)	198.5	(7.4)
93	206.3	(1.8)	228.3	(1.6)	219.3	(3.0)	208.3	(2.8)	219.1	(4.5)	193.2	(2.7)
94	203.6	(1.3)	226.3	(0.9)	215.8	(1.6)	209.1	0.4	218.3	(0.4)	195.8	1.3

Year	S. West		S. East.		Gr. London		Wales		Scotland		N. Ireland	
	Index	%	Index	%	Index	%	Index	%	Index	%	Index	%
87	158.1	20.2	181.0	25.4	200.6	25.7	130.4	10.2	126.8	5.8	121.5	0.1
88	217.6	37.6	232.4	28.4	245.3	22.3	162.3	24.5	139.7	10.2	126.7	4.2
89	242.7	11.5	244.3	5.1	251.1	2.3	215.5	32.8	165.0	18.1	130.6	3.1
90	221.8	(8.6)	224.5	(8.1)	236.6	(5.8)	219.6	1.9	182.1	10.4	132.1	1.1
91	210.4	(5.0)	210.8	(6.1)	222.9	(5.8)	217.1	(1.1)	192.8	5.9	146.9	11.2
92	193.9	(7.8)	192.8	(8.5)	202.0	(9.4)	207.7	(4.3)	193.2	0.2	145.5	(1.0)
93	185.9	(4.1)	186.4	(3.3)	192.0	(4.9)	204.5	(1.6)	196.4	1.6	151.7	4.3
94	188.6	1.5	189.8	1.8	195.5	1.8	201.9	(1.2)	199.4	1.6	162.1	6.9

Index 1983 = 100
% = Percentage change in index from preceding year
Figures in brackets indicate a fall in the index
Region = Economic planning region

The Index is calculated by reference to transactions involving a limited number of carefully chosen individual properties, whereas the average price is a crude figure calculated from the building society's new mortgage business in each period and region. There is thus no correlation between the movements in the Index and the changes in average prices, and the Index is the measure to be relied upon in making comparisons.

Table 13 Valuing Shares

This table may be used in order to achieve a very rough estimate of the value of a shareholding in a private family company: that it produces only a general guideline figure should be emphasised.

The formula used is
   a Maintainable future post-tax profits
× **b** P/E ratio on FT-Actuaries Index for relevant industry sector or on FT-SE-Actuaries All-Share Index (consult current *Financial Times* or a stockbroker)
× **c** Percentage interest in the company
× **d** Adjustment for size of company, size of shareholding, marketability and lack of dividend in accordance with the table *below*

It is very important to note that capital gains tax would notionally be payable on any gain in real value since acquisition (or since March 1982 if later).

Any such latent tax must be calculated and subtracted from the gross figure given by the formula. Table 22 will prove helpful in establishing the amount of capital gains tax, although where the shares were held at March 1982 it may be necessary to undertake a further valuation as at that time.

For the full text of the article upon which this table is based see *Between Scylla and Charybdis: How to value, very broadly, shares in the family company* [1993] Fam Law 113.

Post-tax profit (£'000)					
Size of shareholding	**under 100**	**100–200**	**200–500**	**500–1,000**	**over 1,000**
under 10%	25%	30%	35%	40%	40%
10% to 25%	30%	40%	45%	50%	50%
25.1% to 49.9%	35%	45%	50%	60%	65%
50%	40%	50%	60%	70%	75%
50.1% to 74.9%	45%	55%	65%	75%	85%
75% and over	55%	65%	80%	90%	100%

Worked example

The husband owns 60% of a computer/electronics company. There is no reason to expect a significant variation in the future pattern of profitability, and the profits represent a reasonable return on capital employed in the business.

The recent profit record, before exceptional items and after a normal tax charge, is

1991	£106,000
1992	£72,000
1993	£85,000

The simple average over these years is £87,667. This figure, being higher than the most recent year's profit, is therefore taken to establish maintainable future profits.

On consulting the *Financial Times* it is found that the electronics sector of the FT-Actuaries Index and the FT-SE-Actuaries All-Share Index show historic P/E ratios of 14.50 and 14.64 respectively.

A rough estimate of the husband's interest in the company is therefore

   a £87,667
× **b** say 14.50 = £1,271,151
× **c** 60% = £762,702
× **d** 45% = £343,216

or say **£350,000** to the nearest £25,000.

Table 14 Endowment Premiums

With-profits endowment: monthly premium for a male, sum assured plus any attaching bonuses payable on survival to the end of the term or on earlier death

Age	Term in years								
	10	15	20	25	30	35	40	45	50
20	450.50	294.83	213.83	162.50	128.50	106.00	89.50	77.83	67.50
25	450.50	294.83	213.83	162.50	129.00	107.00	91.33	80.67	71.50
30	450.50	294.83	214.17	163.50	130.67	109.67	95.33	86.00	78.83
35	450.67	295.83	215.83	166.00	134.33	114.83	102.17	95.17	90.00
40	452.17	298.00	219.17	170.67	140.83	123.67	113.67	109.17	106.17
45	455.00	302.33	225.00	178.83	151.83	137.67	130.83		
50	460.00	309.50	235.00	192.33	169.17				
55	468.17	321.33	251.17	213.50					
60	481.33	340.33	276.67	245.83					
65	502.00	370.17	316.00	293.50					

These monthly premiums are for a sum assured of £50,000 based on figures quoted by The Equitable Life in February 1995.

Monthly premium charged is in proportion with the sum assured.
For example, the monthly premium for a sum assured of £75,000 for a male aged 25 over a 30 year term would be £129.00 (see table) × (£75,000÷£50,000) = £129.00 × 1.5 = £193.50.

The above age is applied to males. Females can use the above table noting that female age is equivalent to the male age less four years.

Low-cost endowment: monthly premium for a male, sum assured plus any attaching bonuses on survival to the end of the term, or a guaranteed death benefit on earlier death

Age	Term in years					
	10	15	20	25	30	35
20	346.00	199.83	128.67	87.17	62.33	47.50
25	346.00	199.83	128.67	87.17	62.67	47.83
30	346.00	199.83	128.83	87.67	63.50	49.00
35	346.33	200.67	129.83	89.50	66.17	52.83
40	348.00	202.50	132.83	93.83	71.83	60.33
45	351.17	207.17	139.00	101.83	82.17	72.67
50	356.33	214.83	149.33	115.17	98.33	
55	365.17	227.33	165.83	135.83		
60	379.17	247.33	191.83			
65	401.33	278.67				

The above monthly premiums are for a guaranteed death benefit of £50,000 based on figures quoted by The Equitable Life in February 1995.

Monthly premium charged is in proportion with the guaranteed death benefit.
For example, the monthly premium for a guaranteed death benefit of £30,000 for a male aged 35 over a 25 year term would be £89.50 (see table) × (£30,000÷£50,000) = £89.50 × 0.6 = £53.70.

The above age is applied to males. Females can use the above table noting that female age is equivalent to the male age less four years.

Table 15   Mortgage Repayments

This table shows the initial annual cost in 1995-96 of a repayment mortgage after allowable tax relief

25 year term

Initial borrowing	Mortgage interest rate										
	5%	6%	7%	8%	9%	10%	11%	12%	13%	14%	15%
10,000	635	692	753	817	883	952	1,022	1,095	1,169	1,245	1,322
20,000	1,269	1,385	1,506	1,634	1,766	1,903	2,045	2,190	2,339	2,490	2,644
30,000	1,904	2,077	2,259	2,450	2,649	2,855	3,067	3,285	3,508	3,735	3,966
40,000	2,613	2,859	3,117	3,387	3,667	3,957	4,255	4,560	4,872	5,190	5,513
50,000	3,323	3,641	3,976	4,324	4,685	5,058	5,442	5,835	6,236	6,645	7,060
60,000	4,032	4,424	4,834	5,261	5,703	6,160	6,629	7,110	7,601	8,100	8,607
70,000	4,742	5,206	5,692	6,198	6,721	7,262	7,817	8,385	8,965	9,555	10,154
80,000	5,451	5,988	6,550	7,134	7,740	8,363	9,004	9,660	10,329	11,010	11,701
90,000	6,161	6,770	7,408	8,071	8,758	9,465	10,192	10,935	11,693	12,465	13,248
100,000	6,870	7,553	8,266	9,008	9,776	10,567	11,379	12,210	13,058	13,920	14,795
150,000	10,418	11,464	12,557	13,692	14,866	16,075	17,316	18,585	19,879	21,195	22,530
200,000	13,965	15,375	16,847	18,376	19,956	21,584	23,253	24,960	26,700	28,470	30,265

20 year term

Initial borrowing	Mortgage interest rate										
	5%	6%	7%	8%	9%	10%	11%	12%	13%	14%	15%
10,000	727	782	839	899	960	1,025	1,091	1,159	1,229	1,300	1,373
20,000	1,455	1,564	1,678	1,797	1,921	2,049	2,182	2,318	2,457	2,600	2,745
30,000	2,182	2,346	2,517	2,696	2,881	3,074	3,272	3,476	3,686	3,900	4,118
40,000	2,985	3,217	3,461	3,714	3,977	4,248	4,528	4,815	5,109	5,409	5,715
50,000	3,787	4,089	4,405	4,733	5,072	5,423	5,784	6,154	6,533	6,919	7,313
60,000	4,590	4,961	5,349	5,751	6,168	6,598	7,040	7,493	7,956	8,429	8,911
70,000	5,392	5,833	6,293	6,770	7,263	7,772	8,295	8,832	9,380	9,939	10,508
80,000	6,194	6,705	7,236	7,788	8,359	8,947	9,551	10,170	10,803	11,449	12,106
90,000	6,997	7,577	8,180	8,807	9,454	10,121	10,807	11,509	12,227	12,959	13,704
100,000	7,799	8,448	9,124	9,825	10,550	11,296	12,063	12,848	13,650	14,469	15,301
150,000	11,811	12,808	13,844	14,918	16,027	17,169	18,341	19,542	20,768	22,018	23,289
200,000	15,824	17,167	18,564	20,010	21,504	23,042	24,620	26,236	27,886	29,567	31,277

15 year term

Initial borrowing	Mortgage interest rate										
	5%	6%	7%	8%	9%	10%	11%	12%	13%	14%	15%
10,000	888	940	993	1,048	1,106	1,165	1,226	1,288	1,352	1,418	1,485
20,000	1,777	1,879	1,986	2,097	2,211	2,329	2,451	2,576	2,705	2,836	2,970
30,000	2,665	2,819	2,979	3,145	3,317	3,494	3,677	3,865	4,057	4,254	4,456
40,000	3,629	3,849	4,077	4,313	4,557	4,809	5,068	5,333	5,605	5,882	6,166
50,000	4,592	4,878	5,175	5,481	5,798	6,124	6,458	6,801	7,152	7,510	7,876
60,000	5,556	5,908	6,273	6,650	7,039	7,438	7,849	8,269	8,700	9,139	9,586
70,000	6,519	6,937	7,371	7,818	8,279	8,753	9,240	9,738	10,247	10,767	11,296
80,000	7,482	7,967	8,469	8,986	9,520	10,068	10,630	11,206	11,794	12,395	13,006
90,000	8,446	8,997	9,567	10,155	10,760	11,383	12,021	12,674	13,342	14,023	14,717
100,000	9,409	10,026	10,664	11,323	12,001	12,697	13,412	14,142	14,889	15,651	16,427
150,000	14,226	15,174	16,154	17,164	18,204	19,271	20,365	21,484	22,626	23,791	24,978
200,000	19,043	20,323	21,644	23,006	24,407	25,845	27,318	28,825	30,363	31,932	33,528

Allowance has been made for 15% tax relief on interest upon the first £30,000 borrowed. The net annual cost increases progressively over the mortgage term as the capital outstanding decreases. Thus the interest payable and the tax relief referable thereto both reduce each year.

Illustrations of the increasing percentage of principal repayment (over a 25 year term) are shown *opposite*.

Table 15   Mortgage Repayments

The percentage (%) of net payment in 1995-96 which is principal over a 25 year term

Year	£10,000	£20,000	£30,000	£40,000	£50,000	£60,000
1	16.75	16.75	16.75	16.15	15.82	15.60
2	18.05	18.05	18.05	17.45	17.08	16.85
3	19.45	19.45	19.45	18.84	18.45	18.20
4	20.96	20.96	20.96	20.35	19.93	19.65
5	22.58	22.58	22.58	21.98	21.52	21.23
6	24.32	24.32	24.32	23.74	23.24	22.92
7	26.19	26.19	26.19	25.63	25.10	24.76
8	28.20	28.20	28.20	27.68	27.11	26.74
9	30.35	30.35	30.35	29.90	29.28	28.88
10	32.66	32.66	32.66	32.29	31.62	31.19
11	35.13	35.13	35.13	34.87	34.15	33.68
12	37.78	37.78	37.78	37.66	36.88	36.38
13	40.62	40.62	40.62	40.62	39.83	39.29
14	43.66	43.66	43.66	43.66	43.02	42.43
15	46.91	46.91	46.91	46.91	46.46	45.82
16	50.38	50.38	50.38	50.38	50.18	49.49
17	54.08	54.08	54.08	54.08	54.08	53.45
18	58.03	58.03	58.03	58.03	58.03	57.72
19	62.24	62.24	62.24	62.24	62.24	62.24
20	66.72	66.72	66.72	66.72	66.72	66.72
21	71.48	71.48	71.48	71.48	71.48	71.48
22	76.55	76.55	76.55	76.55	76.55	76.55
23	81.92	81.92	81.92	81.92	81.92	81.92
24	87.61	87.61	87.61	87.61	87.61	87.61
25	93.63	93.63	93.63	93.63	93.63	93.63

Year	£70,000	£80,000	£90,000	£100,000	£150,000	£200,000
1	15.45	15.34	15.25	15.19	14.99	14.89
2	16.69	16.57	16.47	16.40	16.18	16.08
3	18.02	17.89	17.79	17.71	17.48	17.37
4	19.46	19.32	19.21	19.13	18.88	18.75
5	21.02	20.87	20.75	20.66	20.39	20.25
6	22.70	22.54	22.41	22.31	22.02	21.88
7	24.52	24.34	24.20	24.10	23.78	23.63
8	26.48	26.29	26.14	26.03	25.68	25.52
9	28.60	28.39	28.23	28.11	27.74	27.56
10	30.88	30.66	30.49	30.36	29.96	29.76
11	33.36	33.11	32.93	32.78	32.35	32.14
12	36.02	35.76	35.56	35.41	34.94	34.71
13	38.91	38.63	38.41	38.24	37.74	37.49
14	42.02	41.72	41.48	41.30	40.76	40.49
15	45.38	45.05	44.80	44.60	44.02	43.73
16	49.01	48.66	48.39	48.17	47.54	47.23
17	52.93	52.55	52.26	52.02	51.34	51.00
18	57.17	56.75	56.44	56.19	55.45	55.09
19	61.74	61.29	60.95	60.68	59.88	59.49
20	66.68	66.20	65.83	65.54	64.67	64.25
21	71.48	71.48	71.09	70.78	69.85	69.39
22	76.55	76.55	76.55	76.44	75.44	74.94
23	81.92	81.92	81.92	81.92	81.47	80.94
24	87.61	87.61	87.61	87.61	87.61	87.41
25	93.63	93.63	93.63	93.63	93.63	93.63

All calculations are based on net payments, at a mortgage rate of 8.00% with MIRAS available on the first £30,000, and assume tax relief at 15% for 1995-96.

For any two mortgages with the same rate of interest under £30,000 (debt outstanding) the element of principal in any given year will be the same.

For further information contact the Group Planning and Research Department of the Halifax Building Society by telephoning 01422 333333.

Table 16   Value of Lost Pension

A divorce will usually cause a woman to lose the chance of acquiring widow's benefits from her husband's pension. Under s.25 (2) (h) of the Matrimonial Causes Act 1973, these lost benefits are to be taken into account, but often the court either disregards them as 'too remote' or invokes them to justify an otherwise unsustainable award.

Actuarial techniques can be used to estimate the value of these potentially lost pension rights. The approach is to work out the widow's pension based on the husband's current pensionable salary and his expected length of service, and then to adjust the resulting figure to give the prima facie lump sum to be paid to the wife by way of compensation for the loss of that benefit. The adjustment is in the form of two multipliers.

The first multiplier (Table A *opposite*) is the cost at the husband's normal retirement date of buying £1 of widow's pension payable to her on the death of her husband after retirement. There are two factors that affect the first multiplier: the age difference between husband and wife, and the possibility that the pension scheme allows for increase in pensions once in payment. The multipliers in Table A cater for three pension scheme situations: 0% p.a. (i.e. no increases in payment), 3% p.a. and 5% p.a.

The second multiplier (Table B *opposite*) compensates for the payment of the lump sum **now** rather than on the husband's normal retirement date. This discount multiplier takes into account not only expected income and capital growth from such a lump sum, but also expected increases in the husband's earnings, and makes allowance for the possibility of both husband and wife dying before retirement.

In summary:

Prima facie lump sum = Widow's pension ×
Table A multiplier ×
Table B multiplier

For full text and formulae used in compiling these tables, see *What price a widow's mite?* (1991) Fam Law 8.

The assumptions

Husband's retirement date is his 65th birthday: if he retires on his 60th birthday, a rough adjustment would be to work the calculations based on his years of service to age 60, apply the multipliers from Tables A and B unadjusted, but then **increase** the resulting figure by 20%.

No account has been taken of taxation.

Effect of the pension scheme being used to contract husband out of the state scheme is ignored.

Benefits that may be payable on husband's death in service are ignored.

Husband will receive salary increases not markedly out of line with the rate for non-manual workers.

Husband and wife both in good health (if husband in poor health, value of lost benefit will be **greater**; if wife in poor health, **smaller**).

Table 16 Value of Lost Pension

Table A

Husband's age minus wife's age	Multiplier 1 Pension increases in payment at		
	0% p.a.	3% p.a.	5% p.a.
10	2.71	4.45	6.37
9	2.64	4.30	6.12
8	2.57	4.15	5.86
7	2.49	3.99	5.60
6	2.42	3.84	5.35
5	2.34	3.68	5.09
4	2.26	3.52	4.84
3	2.17	3.36	4.59
2	2.09	3.20	4.34
1	2.01	3.05	4.10
0	1.92	2.89	3.86
−1	1.84	2.73	3.62
−2	1.75	2.58	3.39
−3	1.66	2.43	3.17
−4	1.58	2.28	2.96
−5	1.49	2.14	2.75

Table B

Age of husband	Multiplier 2	Age of husband	Multiplier 2
25	0.23	45	0.43
26	0.24	46	0.45
27	0.25	47	0.46
28	0.26	48	0.48
29	0.26	49	0.49
30	0.27	50	0.51
31	0.28	51	0.53
32	0.29	52	0.55
33	0.30	53	0.57
34	0.31	54	0.59
35	0.32	55	0.62
36	0.33	56	0.64
37	0.34	57	0.67
38	0.35	58	0.70
39	0.36	59	0.73
40	0.37	60	0.77
41	0.38	61	0.81
42	0.39	62	0.85
43	0.41	63	0.89
44	0.42	64	0.94

Worked example: male retiring at 65

H is 52 and W is 48. H has 15 years pensionable service to date and will have 28 on normal retirement date (when 65). H's current salary is £24,000. Scheme provides for 1/60th of final salary for each service year and a widow's pension on his death after retirement of 50% of the member's pension. All pensions increase by 3% p.a. in payment.

His expected pension at retirement aged 65, based on current salary, is
    28/60 × £24,000 = **£11,200 p.a.**

The widow's pension, on this basis, is
    50% × £11,200 = **£5,600 p.a.**

Table A multiplier for age difference (H−W) = (52−48) = 4 years and a pension with 3% increase is **3.52**

Table B multiplier for a man aged 52 is **0.55**

Hence an estimate for the prima facie lump sum to be paid by way of compensation is

Widow's pension × Table A multiplier × Table B multiplier

£5,600 × 3.52 × 0.55 = **£10,842**

Table 17   Annuity Rates

Gross annuity for each £1,000 of purchase money payable monthly in advance to a female for her life

Age	Escalating at 0% p.a.		Escalating at 3% p.a.		Escalating at 5% p.a.	
	Gross payment	Capital content	Gross payment	Capital content	Gross payment	Capital content
30	61.92	19.08	36.72	8.04	21.96	4.08
35	63.12	21.00	38.28	9.00	23.88	5.04
40	64.68	23.04	40.32	11.04	26.16	6.00
45	66.96	26.04	43.08	13.08	29.04	8.04
50	69.96	30.00	46.56	16.08	32.76	10.08
55	74.04	34.08	51.24	20.04	37.56	14.04
60	80.04	40.08	57.60	26.04	44.16	19.08
65	88.56	49.08	66.36	33.00	52.92	25.08

Notes

1 The rates quoted are not guaranteed. They are subject to market fluctuations and are sensitive to interest rates. The table shows rates supplied by The Equitable Life on 16 February 1995. Quotations for more sophisticated annuities (e.g. index-linked, with profits, guaranteed for a minimum term of years) are available in the market.

2 The tables make no allowance for income tax on the taxable element (the gross payment less the capital content), which for each annuitant will depend on relevant personal circumstances: see Table 20.

3 Intervening ages can be approximately interpolated. For male annuitants the tables can be applied by adopting the figures for a female about 4 years older than the male in question.

Table 18 Life Expectancy

Further life expectancy in years according to age and sex

	Male							Female							
	20	**30**	**40**	**50**	**60**	**70**	**80**	**20**	**30**	**40**	**50**	**60**	**70**	**80**	
0	52	43	33	24	16	10	6	58	48	39	29	21	13	7	**0**
1	52	42	32	23	16	10	5	57	47	38	29	20	13	7	**1**
2	51	41	31	23	15	9	5	56	46	37	28	19	12	7	**2**
3	50	40	31	22	14	9	5	55	45	36	27	19	11	6	**3**
4	49	39	30	21	14	8	5	54	44	35	26	18	11	6	**4**
5	48	38	29	20	13	8	4	53	43	34	25	17	10	5	**5**
6	47	37	28	19	12	7	4	52	43	33	24	16	10	5	**6**
7	46	36	27	19	12	7	4	51	42	32	23	16	9	5	**7**
8	45	35	26	18	11	6	4	50	41	31	23	15	9	4	**8**
9	44	34	25	17	11	6	4	49	40	30	22	14	8	4	**9**

Notes

To find life expectancy choose column according to sex, and age in tens of years:
then look down to find appropriate row according to units of years.

Example: for a 33-year-old **Female**, look to the intersection of **30** column and **3** row to find figure of 45: this gives the actuarial expectation of death at the age of 78 (33 + 45).

Caveat

This Table follows *English Life Tables No.14* (ELT14) prepared by the Government Actuary, based on statistics for the general population of England and Wales from 1980-82. It will be revised in about two years' time, and is somewhat outdated (although still the best available for the population as a whole) because mortality expectations have changed for the better. Note that the life expectancy of professional people is in any event greater than for the general population.

The life expectancy column in the **Duxbury Calculations** (Table 19) reflects the more optimistic life table PA90. This is prepared by the Faculty & Institute of Actuaries based on statistics for pensioners in insured pension schemes, whose life expectancy as a group is also greater than that of the population taken as a whole. **Duxbury** funds calculated using PA90 thus produce higher capital requirements (by about 2% to 8%) than if ELT14 were adopted as their basis.

The argument for the choice of PA90 is that the recipient of a **Duxbury** award is more likely to be (or to become) as healthy, stress-free and long-living as the pensioners in insured pension schemes whose statistics contributed to that table, as compared with the general population.

Table 19 Duxbury Calculations

Capitalising maintenance: capital required (to nearest £1,000) to fund a wife's net income need for life

Age of wife	Life expectancy	£10,000	£12,000	£14,000	£16,000	£18,000	£20,000	£25,000
42	39	177,000	220,000	263,000	307,000	351,000	394,000	503,000
43	38	174,000	216,000	259,000	302,000	345,000	388,000	496,000
44	37	170,000	212,000	255,000	297,000	339,000	382,000	488,000
45	36	167,000	208,000	250,000	292,000	333,000	375,000	480,000
46	35	163,000	204,000	245,000	286,000	327,000	368,000	471,000
47	34	160,000	200,000	240,000	281,000	321,000	362,000	463,000
48	33	156,000	195,000	235,000	275,000	315,000	354,000	454,000
49	32	152,000	191,000	230,000	269,000	308,000	347,000	445,000
50	31	148,000	186,000	224,000	263,000	301,000	339,000	435,000
51	31	146,000	184,000	223,000	261,000	299,000	338,000	434,000
52	30	142,000	179,000	217,000	254,000	292,000	330,000	424,000
53	29	138,000	174,000	211,000	248,000	285,000	322,000	414,000
54	28	133,000	169,000	205,000	241,000	277,000	313,000	403,000
55	27	129,000	164,000	199,000	234,000	269,000	304,000	393,000
56	26	124,000	158,000	192,000	227,000	261,000	295,000	381,000
57	25	119,000	152,000	186,000	219,000	253,000	286,000	370,000
58	24	114,000	146,000	179,000	211,000	244,000	277,000	358,000
59	23	109,000	140,000	172,000	203,000	235,000	267,000	346,000
60	23	106,000	138,000	170,000	201,000	233,000	265,000	344,000
62	21	100,000	130,000	159,000	189,000	219,000	248,000	323,000
64	19	93,000	121,000	148,000	176,000	203,000	231,000	300,000
66	18	90,000	116,000	142,000	169,000	195,000	222,000	288,000
68	16	82,000	106,000	130,000	154,000	179,000	203,000	264,000
70	15	78,000	101,000	124,000	147,000	170,000	193,000	251,000
72	13	70,000	90,000	111,000	131,000	152,000	172,000	224,000
74	12	65,000	85,000	104,000	123,000	142,000	161,000	210,000
76	11	61,000	79,000	96,000	114,000	132,000	150,000	195,000

In **B v B** [1990] 1 FLR 20 Ward J stated, at page 24E-G: 'The Duxbury calculation was conceived to address the observations of the Court of Appeal in **Preston v Preston** [1982] Fam 17. There the Court of Appeal pointed out firstly that the recipient of the lump sum is expected to expend it, or so much of it as is intended to meet future income needs, by drawing both upon its capital as well as relying upon the income it can produce. Secondly, that help should be provided to the court by accountants or investment consultants, or even by reference to annuity tables, to show the court how the lump sum could be thus applied. As a result of Preston the practice has grown up for accountants to devise a computer program which can calculate the lump sum which, if invested on the assumptions as to life expectancy, rates of inflation, return on investment, growth of capital, incidence of income tax, will produce enough to meet the recipient's needs for her life . . . I have concluded that, if this calculation is accepted as no more than a tool for the judge's use, then it is a very valuable help to him in many cases'.

In **Gojkovic v Gojkovic** [1992] Fam 40, Butler-Sloss LJ stated, at page 48E:
'. . . a Duxbury calculation cannot by itself provide the answer as to the sum to which the wife is entitled, though it produces a figure to which the judge is entitled to have regard in deciding what is the right answer'.

In **Vicary v Vicary** [1992] 2 FLR 271, Purchas LJ said, at page 278B:
'Whilst acknowledging that in the negotiation process . . . Duxbury calculations are obviously useful as guidelines, I must emphasise that there is a danger of such an approach achieving a status far beyond that which it ever had in the [Duxbury] case. . . . It certainly should never be allowed to derogate in any way from the wide discretion of the court to take into account all the circumstances of the case as required in s.25 of the Act.'

Table 19   Duxbury Calculations

£30,000	£35,000	£40,000	£50,000	£60,000	£80,000	£100,000	Life expectancy	Age of wife
612,000	723,000	838,000	1,074,000	1,313,000	1,793,000	2,274,000	39	42
603,000	712,000	825,000	1,057,000	1,292,000	1,765,000	2,239,000	38	43
594,000	701,000	812,000	1,040,000	1,271,000	1,736,000	2,202,000	37	44
584,000	689,000	798,000	1,022,000	1,249,000	1,706,000	2,165,000	36	45
574,000	678,000	784,000	1,004,000	1,227,000	1,676,000	2,127,000	35	46
564,000	666,000	770,000	985,000	1,204,000	1,645,000	2,087,000	34	47
553,000	653,000	755,000	966,000	1,181,000	1,613,000	2,047,000	33	48
543,000	640,000	740,000	947,000	1,157,000	1,581,000	2,006,000	32	49
531,000	627,000	725,000	927,000	1,133,000	1,547,000	1,964,000	31	50
530,000	626,000	723,000	925,000	1,131,000	1,546,000	1,962,000	31	51
518,000	612,000	707,000	905,000	1,106,000	1,512,000	1,919,000	30	52
506,000	598,000	691,000	884,000	1,080,000	1,477,000	1,874,000	29	53
493,000	584,000	674,000	862,000	1,050,000	1,441,000	1,829,000	28	54
481,000	569,000	657,000	840,000	1,027,000	1,404,000	1,782,000	27	55
467,000	554,000	640,000	817,000	999,000	1,366,000	1,734,000	26	56
454,000	538,000	622,000	794,000	971,000	1,327,000	1,685,000	25	57
440,000	521,000	603,000	770,000	941,000	1,287,000	1,635,000	24	58
425,000	505,000	584,000	746,000	911,000	1,246,000	1,583,000	23	59
423,000	502,000	582,000	744,000	910,000	1,244,000	1,581,000	23	60
397,000	471,000	546,000	697,000	851,000	1,163,000	1,478,000	21	62
369,000	439,000	508,000	647,000	789,000	1,078,000	1,369,000	19	64
355,000	421,000	488,000	621,000	757,000	1,034,000	1,312,000	18	66
325,000	385,000	446,000	568,000	691,000	942,000	1,194,000	16	68
309,000	367,000	424,000	540,000	657,000	894,000	1,134,000	15	70
275,000	327,000	379,000	482,000	585,000	795,000	1,007,000	13	72
258,000	306,000	355,000	451,000	548,000	743,000	941,000	12	74
240,000	285,000	330,000	420,000	510,000	691,000	874,000	11	76

The assumptions

The columns in the Table relate to an initial annual net income requirement for the wife, calculated after tax at 1995-96 rates. The Table assumes that the wife has no other income (save the state pension from age 60).

The figures in the Table assume an income yield of 4.25%, capital growth of 2%, and inflation of 2%. Thus the assumed real rate of return is 4.25% (being the difference between inflation rate and the sum of the rates for income yield and capital growth).

For a discussion of the reasons why this edition adopts 4.25% as the real rate of return, and a plea for an end to over-refinement in these calculations, see the **Reflections** at page iv.

The computer program increases the annual budget for inflation on an annual rather than a continuous basis. By contrast the income yield for each year is computed upon the average of the opening and closing capital for the year and thus assumes that capital growth is linear.

The program permits other variables to be introduced, such as earned income and external capital receipts, whether now or at some future known or postulated date. Foreign tax environments can be accommodated. Such factors cannot be demonstrated in tabular form, and where they arise bespoke calculations should be obtained.

The **Life expectancy** column reflects life table PA90 for the reasons set out in the **Caveat** to Table 18.

Table 20   Income Tax

	Fiscal year						
	89-90	**90-91**	**91-92**	**92-93**	**93-94**	**94-95**	**95-96**
Income Tax Rates							
20% on first taxable				2,000	2,500	3,000	3,200
25% on first taxable/next	20,700	20,700	23,700	21,700	21,200	20,700	21,100
and 40% on excess over	20,700	20,700	23,700	23,700	23,700	23,700	24,300
Income Tax Reliefs							
Personal allowance	—	3,005	3,295	3,445	3,445	3,445	3,525
Married couple's allowance	—	1,720	1,720	1,720	1,720	1,720*	1,720*
Previous personal allowances							
Single	2,785	—	—	—	—	—	—
Married	4,375	—	—	—	—	—	—
Wife's earned income							
allowance	2,785	—	—	—	—	—	—
Additional personal allowance	1,590	1,720	1,720	1,720	1,720	1,720*	1,720*
Age allowances							
For age 65 to 74							
Personal allowance	—	3,670	4,020	4,200	4,200	4,200	4,630
Married couple's allowance	—	2,145	2,355	2,465	2,465	2,655*	2,995*
Previous personal							
allowances							
Single	3,400	—	—	—	—	—	—
Married	5,385	—	—	—	—	—	—
For age 75 and over							
Personal allowance	—	3,820	4,180	4,370	4,370	4,370	4,800
Married couple's allowance	—	2,185	2,395	2,505	2,505	2,705*	3,035*
Previous personal							
allowances							
Single	3,540	—	—	—	—	—	—
Married	5,565	—	—	—	—	—	—
Income limit	11,400	12,300	13,500	14,200	14,200	14,200	14,600

*Relief limited to 20% for 1994-95; and to 15% for 1995-96.

Table 21   Inheritance Tax

Cumulative transfers exceeding £154,000 (for deaths on or after 6 April 1995) taxed at 40%.

Potentially exempt transfers between three and seven years prior to death taxed at tapering rates.

Transfers more than seven years prior to death usually exempt.

£3,000 annual exemption for chargeable lifetime transfers.

Table 22 Capital Gains Tax Rates and Indexation

To permit approximate calculation of the latent CGT relating to assets owned prior to March 1982 or acquired since that date

Year	Jan	Feb	Mar	Apr	May	Jun	Jul	Aug	Sep	Oct	Nov	Dec
82			1.838	1.802	1.789	1.784	1.783	1.783	1.784	1.775	1.766	1.769
83	1.767	1.760	1.756	1.732	1.725	1.721	1.712	1.704	1.696	1.691	1.685	1.680
84	1.681	1.674	1.669	1.647	1.641	1.637	1.639	1.623	1.620	1.610	1.605	1.607
85	1.601	1.588	1.573	1.540	1.533	1.530	1.533	1.529	1.530	1.527	1.528	1.520
86	1.517	1.511	1.509	1.495	1.492	1.493	1.497	1.493	1.485	1.483	1.470	1.466
87	1.460	1.454	1.451	1.434	1.433	1.433	1.434	1.430	1.426	1.419	1.412	1.413
88	1.413	1.408	1.402	1.380	1.375	1.370	1.368	1.353	1.347	1.333	1.327	1.324
89	1.315	1.306	1.300	1.277	1.270	1.265	1.264	1.261	1.252	1.243	1.232	1.229
90	1.222	1.214	1.203	1.167	1.156	1.152	1.151	1.140	1.129	1.120	1.123	1.124
91	1.121	1.115	1.111	1.097	1.093	1.088	1.091	1.089	1.085	1.081	1.077	1.076
92	1.077	1.071	1.068	1.052	1.048	1.048	1.052	1.051	1.047	1.044	1.045	1.049
93	1.059	1.052	1.048	1.038	1.035	1.035	1.038	1.033	1.029	1.030	1.031	1.029
94	1.033	1.027	1.025	1.012	1.009	1.009	1.010	1.009	1.007	1.006	1.005	1.000

Worked example for disposal (or notional disposal) in December 1994

The rules state that the indexation date is March 1982 or that of the month of acquisition, whichever is the later.

If a husband bought shares for £10,000 in March 1984 the indexation factor taken is 1.669. The uplifted base value is therefore £16,690.

If the shares are worth £50,000 in December 1994 then the taxable gain will be £33,310.

If the husband's annual exemption of £5,800 (for 1994-95; for 1995-96 see **Rates** *below*) is already fully utilised and his marginal rate of income tax is 40% then the notional tax is £13,324 giving the shares a net value of £36,676.

In **O'D v O'D** [1976] Fam 83 Ormrod LJ stated that capital gains tax on a notional disposal of the husband's assets should be taken into account 'to place the husband in approximately the right position on the scale of wealth'. This table enables this exercise to be performed without the use of the formula in the Retail Price Index table (Table 1).

It must be noted that this table is accurate for disposals (or notional disposals) in the month of December 1994, as the factors are calculated by reference to the RPI figure prevailing at that date. Hence as (or if) inflation progresses they will become slightly inaccurate.

Capital Gains Tax Rates

Gains are taxed at the individual's marginal rate of income tax: see Table 20 *opposite.*

Indexation relief is first deducted from the gain since value at March 1982 or (if later) cost at the acquisition date: see **Worked example** *above.*

For 1995-96 the first £6,000 of gains are exempt: the limit for 1994-95 was £5,800.

Table 23 Social Security Benefits (Non-means-tested)

A. Income replacement

1. *Retirement*

Retirement Pension	94-95	95-96
Claimant	57.60	58.85
Non-contributing spouse/adult		
dependant - extra	34.50	35.25

Every pensioner aged over 80 receives an additional £0.25 p.w. or £13.00 p.a.

Either spouse may qualify in their own right, or as a dependant.
Special rules apply for married women, divorced people, widows and widowers.
Contributory and taxable.

2. *Ill Health*

i. Statutory Sick Pay	94-95	95-96
Standard rate	52.50	52.50
Lower rate	47.80	n/a

Paid by the employer for 168 days (28 six-day weeks), and taxable.

ii. Sickness Benefit	94-95
Over pension age	55.25
Adult dependant - extra	33.10
Under pension age	43.45
Adult dependant - extra	26.90

Paid for 168 days to claimants not entitled to Statutory Sick Pay. Normally contributory unless as a result of an industrial accident or disease. Non-taxable. Abolished from April 1995.

iii. Invalidity Benefit	94-95	95-96
Invalidity Pension	57.60	n/a
Adult dependant - extra	34.50	n/a
Invalidity Allowance (age-related additions; transitional for 1995-96)		
Higher	12.15	12.40
Middle	7.60	7.80
Lower	3.80	3.90

Paid if incapable of work at the end of 168 days during which Statutory Sick Pay/Sickness Benefit is paid. Normally contributory unless as a result of an industrial accident or disease. Non-taxable. Abolished from April 1995.

A. *(Continued)*

iv. Incapacity Benefit	95-96
Long-term	58.85
Increase for age Higher rate	12.40
Lower rate	6.20
Short-term (under pension age)	
Lower rate	44.40
Higher rate	52.50
Short-term (over pension age)	
Lower & Higher rate	56.45

Incapacity Benefit replaces Sickness Benefit and Invalidity Benefit from April 1995. Eligibility is based on an assessment of functional limitation. Short-term Incapacity Benefit is payable at the lower rate for 1-28 weeks (assessed against own job) and at the higher rate from 29-52 weeks (assessed against any work). Long-term Incapacity Benefit is payable from 52 weeks.
Contributory. Taxable for new claimants for short-term higher rate and long-term benefits only; otherwise non-taxable. Transitional rules preserve tax exemption for existing claimants of abolished benefits.

v. Severe Disablement Allowance	94-95	95-96
Claimant	34.80	35.55
Adult dependant - extra	20.70	21.15
Age-related additions		
Higher	12.15	12.40
Middle	7.60	7.80
Lower	3.80	3.90

Paid if 80% disabled.
Non-contributory and non-taxable.

vi. Invalid Care Allowance	94-95	95-96
Claimant	34.50	35.25
Adult dependant - extra	20.65	21.10

Paid to claimants who care for someone receiving the higher or middle rates of the Care Component of Disability Living Allowance *opposite*.
Non-contributory. Claimant's benefit is taxable; extra benefit for adult dependant is non-taxable.

3. *Unemployment*

Unemployment Benefit	94-95	95-96
Claimant (under pension age)	45.45	46.45
Adult dependant - extra	28.05	28.65

Paid for one year after redundancy.
Contributory and taxable.

Entitlement to contributory benefits depends on payment of National Insurance contributions.
Amounts are per week.

Table 23 Social Security Benefits (Non-means-tested)

A. *(Continued)*

4. *Maternity*

i. Statutory Maternity Pay	94-95	95-96
Higher rate (first 6 weeks)		

i. Statutory Maternity Pay	94-95	95-96
Higher rate (first 6 weeks)	90% of average weekly wage	
Lower rate (next 12 weeks maximum)	48.80	52.50

Paid by the employer for a maximum of 18 weeks. Taxable.

ii. Maternity Allowance	94-95	95-96
Claimant	44.55	45.55
Adult dependant - extra	26.90	27.50

Paid for 18 weeks to claimants not entitled to Statutory Maternity Pay.
Contributory and non-taxable.

5. *Widowhood*

Widow's Benefit	94-95	95-96
Widow's Payment (lump sum)	1,000.00	1,000.00
Widowed Mother's Allowance	57.60	58.85
Widow's Pension (age-related)		
45-54	17.28 to 53.57	17.66 to 54.73
55 or over	57.60	58.85

A different scale applies for deaths before 11 April 1988.
The lump sum widow's payment is contributory and non-taxable.
Weekly benefits are contributory and taxable.

Additional child payments for certain benefits only

	94-95	95-96
Child - extra	11.00	11.05

Paid in addition to long-term Income replacement benefits (Retirement Pension, short-term higher rate and long-term Incapacity Benefit, Severe Disablement Allowance, Invalid Care Allowance, Widowed Mother's Allowance and Widow's Pension) and to short-term lower rate Incapacity Benefit and Unemployment Benefit if claimant over pensionable age. A child must be under 16, or under 19 and in full-time secondary education. Reduced to £9.85 if overlapping Child Benefit also in payment.

B. Special needs

1. *Disability Living Allowance*

		94-95	95-96
Care Component	Higher	45.70	46.70
	Middle	30.55	31.20
	Lower	12.15	12.40
Mobility Component	Higher	31.95	32.65
	Lower	12.15	12.40

The range of allowances is related to need.
Non-contributory and non-taxable.

2. *Attendance Allowance*

	94-95	95-96
Higher rate	45.70	46.70
Lower rate	30.55	31.20

Paid for attendance needs of those over 65.
Non-contributory and non-taxable.

C. Children

1. *Child Benefit*

	94-95	95-96
Only/elder/eldest child	10.20	10.40
Each subsequent child	8.25	8.45

A child must be under 16, or under 19 and in full-time secondary education.
Non-contributory and non-taxable.

2. *One Parent Benefit*

	94-95	95-96
Claimant	6.15	6.30

Non-contributory and non-taxable.

3. *Guardian's Allowance*

	94-95	95-96
Claimant	11.00	11.05

Reduced to £9.85 if overlapping Child Benefit also in payment.
Non-contributory and non-taxable.

Entitlement to contributory benefits depends on payment of National Insurance contributions.
Amounts are per week except for lump sum widow's payment.

Table 24 Social Security Benefits (Means-tested)

Income support

	94-95	95-96	Total 95-96
Personal Allowances			
Single person 18-24	36.15	36.80	1,913.60
25 or over	45.70	46.50	2,418.00
Lone Parent			
Under 18 Usual rate	27.50	28.00	1,456.00
Higher rate	36.15	36.80	1,913.60
Over 18	45.70	46.50	2,418.00
Couple One or both over 18	71.70	73.00	3,796.00
Dependant children Under 11	15.65	15.95	829.40
11-15	23.00	23.40	1,216.80
16-17	27.50	28.00	1,456.00
18	36.15	36.80	1,913.60
Premiums			
Family	10.05	10.25	533.00
Lone parent	5.10	5.20	270.40
Disabled child	19.45	19.80	1,029.60
Carer	12.40	12.60	655.20
Pensioner Single	18.25	18.60	967.20
Couple	27.55	28.05	1,458.60
Pensioner (Enhanced) Single	20.35	20.70	1,076.40
Couple	30.40	30.95	1,609.40
Pensioner (Higher) Single	24.70	25.15	1,307.80
Couple	35.30	35.95	1,869.40
Disability Single	19.45	19.80	1,029.60
Couple	27.80	28.30	1,471.60
Severe Disability	34.30	35.05	1,822.60

A need level is established from the above allowances and premiums, plus mortgage interest on loans of up to £100,000 (new claimants) where applicable, with new restrictions limiting increases during a claim. Income Support is then paid to supplement other income to that level. There are detailed rules on the application of premiums and disregarded income. No disregard for maintenance or child care costs.

Childless people aged under 18 are not usually eligible for Income Support.

A claimant is allowed to work up to 16 hours p.w. while still receiving Income Support.

Available capital affects Income Support. Capital up to £3,000 is disregarded. Capital between £3,000 and £8,000 is deemed to produce tariff income of £1.00 for each £250 over £3,000. There is no entitlement to Income Support if capital exceeds £8,000, not including value of home. Notional capital rules penalise the deliberate deprivation of capital to obtain Income Support.

Non-contributory. Not ordinarily taxable, Income Support is reduced if voluntarily unemployed when it becomes potentially taxable.

Entitlement to Income Support brings automatic entitlement on income grounds to other benefits including maximum Housing Benefit and Council Tax Benefit *opposite*.

Amounts are per week, except for the right-hand column where the 1995-96 annual rate is shown.

Table 24 Social Security Benefits (Means-tested)

Family Credit

		94-95	95-96
Applicable amount		71.70	73.00
Claimant		44.30	45.10
Child credit	Under 11	11.20	11.40
	11-15	18.55	18.90
	16-17	23.05	23.45
	Over 18	32.20	32.80

Paid to top up the wages of people with children. The claimant must have children and work at least 16 hours p.w. If the claimant's net income is the same as or below the applicable amount then the sums shown *above* are paid for the claimant and each relevant child. If net income exceeds the applicable amount 70% of the excess is deducted from Family Credit. Some income (but no earned income) is disregarded, including £15.00 p.w. maintenance. Single parents and working/disabled couples may have up to £40.00 p.w. disregarded for nursery/registered childminding fees.

Capital and notional capital has the same effect as for Income Support *opposite.*

Non-contributory and non-taxable.

Disability Working Allowance

		94-95	95-96
Applicable amount			
Single		43.00	54.75
Couple/Lone parent		71.70	73.00
Claimant Single		46.05	46.85
Couple/Lone parent		63.75	73.40
Child credit	Under 11	11.20	11.40
	11-15	18.55	18.90
	16-17	23.05	23.45
	Over 18	32.20	32.80

Paid to top up low wages for the disabled, Disability Working Allowance works on the same principle as Family Credit *left.*

Capital and notional capital affects Disability Working Allowance. Capital up to £3,000 is disregarded. Capital between £3,000 and £16,000 is deemed to produce tariff income of £1.00 for each £250 over £3,000. There is no entitlement to Disability Working Allowance if capital exceeds £16,000.

Non-contributory and non-taxable.

Housing Benefit and Council Tax Benefit

		94-95	95-96
Claimant	16-24	36.15	36.80
	25 or over	45.70	46.50
Lone Parent	Under 18	36.15	36.80
	18 or over	45.70	46.50
Couple	Both under 18	54.55	55.55
	One or both over 18	71.70	73.00
Dependant children	Under 11	15.65	15.95
	11-15	23.00	23.40
	16-17	27.50	28.00
	18	36.15	36.80

Premiums
As for Income Support *opposite* except

	94-95	95-96
Lone parent	11.25	11.50

Housing Benefit is paid to assist those other than owner-occupiers with housing costs. People under 18 do not pay Council Tax.

There are detailed rules on the application of premiums. Some income is disregarded including £25.00 p.w. of single parent's earnings and £15.00 p.w. maintenance. Disregard for childcare costs as for Family Credit *above.* A similar taper principle to Family Credit *above* applies save that the reduction for any excess of income over allowances and premiums is 65% for Housing Benefit and 20% for Council Tax Benefit, reducing the Benefit from 100% of eligible rent/Council Tax.

Where other adult residents preclude the claimant receiving single person discount, an alternative Council Tax Benefit applies, up to a maximum of 25% of the Council Tax due, based on the income of those other residents.

Capital has the same effect for each Benefit as for Disability Working Allowance *above.* Notional capital rules as for Income Support *left.* Non-contributory and non-taxable.

Amounts are per week.

Table 25 National Insurance Contributions

Class 1 Earnings Limits, and Class 2, Class 3 and Class 4 Limits and Contributions

		1994-95	1995-96
Class 1	Lower earnings limit	£57 p.w.	£58 p.w.
	Upper earnings limit	£430 p.w.	£440 p.w.
Class 2	Flat rate contribution	£5.65 p.w.	£5.75 p.w.
	Small earnings exception limit	£3,200 p.a.	£3,260 p.a.
Class 3	Flat rate voluntary contribution	£5.55 p.w.	£5.65 p.w.
Class 4	Lower profits limit	£6,490 p.a.	£6,640 p.a.
	Upper profits limit	£22,360 p.a.	£22,880 p.a.
	Contribution rate	7.3%	7.3%
	Maximum annual contribution	£1,158.51	£1,185.52

Class 1 earnings limits apply only to employees' primary contributions.

Class 4 (self-employed) contributions are deductible as to half against income tax.

Rates of Class 1 Contributions for 1995-96

Primary contribution (employee)		Secondary contribution (employer)			
Standard rate		Weekly earnings	Not contracted-out rate (applied to all earnings) %	Contracted-out rate (%) (sum of both columns)	
Not contracted-out rate %	Contracted-out rate %			On first £58 p.w.	On excess to £440 p.w.
2% of £58 PLUS 10% of that part of earnings which exceeds £58 but does not exceed £440	2% of £58 PLUS 8.2% of that part of earnings which exceeds £58 but does not exceed £440	up to £58.00	Nil	Nil	Nil
		£58.00 to £104.99	3.0	3.0	Nil
		£105.00 to £149.99	5.0	5.0	2.0
		£150.00 to £204.99	7.0	7.0	4.0
		£205.00 to £440.00	10.2	10.2	7.2
		over £440.00	10.2	£33.42 plus 10.2% of excess over £440	

No contributions are payable by or for those whose earnings do not exceed £57.99 p.w.

The reduced rate for married women and widow optants is 3.85% of earnings up to £440.00 p.w.

Table 26   Gross and Net Pay

Net income derived from gross annual salary for 1995-96

Gross salary (£ per annum)	Net income (£ per annum)	Net as % of gross
5,000	4,362	87.2
7,500	6,069	80.9
10,000	7,683	76.8
12,500	9,297	74.4
15,000	10,911	72.7
17,500	12,524	71.6
20,000	14,138	70.7
22,500	15,752	70.0
25,000	17,540	70.2
27,500	19,359	70.4
30,000	20,986	70.0
32,500	22,441	69.0
35,000	23,896	68.3
37,500	25,351	67.6
40,000	26,806	67.0
45,000	29,716	66.0
50,000	32,626	65.3
55,000	35,536	64.6
60,000	38,446	64.1
65,000	41,356	63.6
70,000	44,266	63.2
80,000	50,086	62.6
90,000	55,906	62.1
100,000	61,726	61.7
125,000	76,276	61.0
150,000	90,826	60.6
175,000	105,376	60.2
200,000	119,926	60.0
250,000	149,026	59.6
300,000	178,126	59.4
350,000	207,226	59.2
400,000	236,326	59.1

Assumptions: 1995-96 tax rates; 3% contributory pension; contracted out of Class 1 NIC.

Table 27   Grossed-up Net Maintenance

The gross-income equivalent of maintenance, and some comparable salaries

Maintenance (£)	Grossed-up equivalent (£)	Comparable gross salaries
4,000	4,479	
5,000	5,920	
6,000	7,393	Student Nurse (£7,339)
7,000	8,942	
8,000	10,491	Army Private Class II Band 1 (£10,581)
9,000	12,041	Deacon (£11,940); Anglican Clergy (£12,800)
10,000	13,590	Staff Nurse (£13,339); Teacher Point 3 (£14,151)
12,500	17,462	Leading Seaman Scale B (£15,530); Army Lieutenant (£17,649)
15,000	21,336	Ward Sister (£20,188); Dean (£20,210)
17,500	24,946	Bishop (£24,950); Head Teacher Point 10 (£27,171)
20,000	28,382	Major after 1 year (£29,353)
22,500	32,602	M.P. (£33,189); Major after 8 years (£34,323)
25,000	36,897	
27,500	41,193	Lieutenant Colonel (£40,381); G.P. (£43,165)
30,000	45,489	Archbishop of Canterbury (£45,350)
32,500	49,784	Parliamentary Under-Secretary (£47,987); Colonel after 4 years (£49,494)
35,000	54,079	Head Teacher Point 51 (£53,559); Minister of State (£55,292)
37,500	58,375	Brigadier (£57,736); Leader of the Opposition (£62,480)
40,000	62,671	District Judge at PRFD (£63,327)
42,500	66,966	Bottom of Civil Service Grade 2 range (£67,500); Secretary of State (£67,819)
45,000	71,262	Circuit Judge (£72,524)
47,500	75,557	
50,000	79,852	Prime Minister (£82,003)
52,500	84,148	Senior Circuit Judge, and Official Referee (£85,241)
55,000	88,443	Bottom of Civil Service Grade 1 range (£90,000)
57,500	92,739	
60,000	97,035	General (£97,430); Top of Civil Service Grade 2 range (£98,000); High Court Judge (£98,957)
62,500	101,330	
65,000	105,626	
67,500	109,921	Lord Justice of Appeal (£110,137)
70,000	114,217	Lord of Appeal, and Master of the Rolls (£114,874)
72,500	118,513	
75,000	122,808	Chief of the Defence Staff (£121,130)
77,500	127,103	Lord Chief Justice (£124,138)
80,000	131,399	Lord Chancellor (£126,138)
		Top of Civil Service Grade 1 range (£150,000)

Assumptions for the grossed-up equivalent: 1995-96 tax rates; 3% contributory pension; contracted out of Class 1 NIC.

The comparable salaries are those current at 1 April 1995, except that nursing salaries assume a full 3% increase at that date, not yet conceded as we go to press.

Terms and conditions for the comparable salaries are various.

Sources: Church Commissioners, Royal College of Nursing, Government Departments.

Table 28   Big Money Awards

This table analyses awards made to the wife in nine notable reported big money clean break cases

Initial award

Case and year decided	Assets (£)	Award (£)	Proportion (%)	Years of marriage
O'D (1974)	215,000	70,000	32.6	12
Page (1980)	388,137	120,000	30.9	41
Preston (1980)	2,350,000	700,000	29.8	23
Duxbury (1984)	2,700,000	750,000	27.8	22
Newton (1988)	2,500,000	750,000	30.0	18
R v R[1] (1988)	10,786,000	2,475,000	22.9	25
E v E[2] (1989)	1,500,000	450,000	30.0	16
Gojkovic[3] (1989)	4,000,000	1,295,000	32.4	17
Vicary[4] (1991)	2,237,000	637,000	28.5	15

Award per year of marriage (adjusted for inflation)

Case and year decided	Adjusted assets (£)	Adjusted award (£)	Award per year of marriage (£)	Years of marriage
O'D (1974)	1,128,731	367,494	30,624	12
Page (1980)	834,457	257,989	6,292	41
Preston (1980)	5,052,275	1,504,933	65,432	23
Duxbury (1984)	4,424,242	1,228,956	55,862	22
Newton (1988)	3,420,806	1,026,242	57,013	18
R v R[1] (1988)	14,758,725	3,386,598	135,464	25
E v E[2] (1989)	1,896,104	568,831	35,552	16
Gojkovic[3] (1989)	5,056,277	1,636,970	96,292	17
Vicary[4] (1991)	2,440,972	695,082	46,339	15

The table demonstrates a uniformity of approach as to the conventional proportion awarded, but reveals considerable inconsistency in attributing weight to the length of the marriage.

It must be remembered that the exercise is essentially one of discretion, and thus the table should not be taken too seriously.

For full case citations see subheading 'Money, big' under **Leading Cases**.

In this edition the inflation uplift has been taken from the year in which the case was decided, rather than reported.

[1] The husband asserted that these assets should be reduced by £3.75m in respect of guarantees given by him referable to potential liabilities.
[2] Over half the award was in trust.
[3] These '17 years of marriage' included nine years premarital cohabitation.
[4] The assets figure takes the mid-point between the parties' respective estimates of the husband's assets.

Tax Relief on Maintenance 1995-96

OLD ORDERS
Orders made on or before 30 June 1988 on applications made before 15 March 1988;
subsequent orders replacing such orders;
agreements made before 15 March 1988.

Payers
Tax relief is pegged to the global amount payable and paid in the tax year 1988-89. No relief is given on any amount in excess of the pegged amount.

Relief is given on the first £1,720 at 15%, with any balance at the payer's marginal rate.

Worked example
H presently pays maintenance of £10,000 p.a. In the tax year 1988-89 he paid £6,720. His income is £23,525.

He receives tax relief as follows:		His tax liability is thus:	
Income	£23,525	Tax: first £3,200 @ 20% =	£640
less personal allowance	(£3,525)	next £11,800 @ 25% =	£2,950
less relief at marginal rate on		less relief on £1,720 @ 15% =	(£258)
£6,720 – £1,720 =	(£5,000)		
		Tax payable	£3,332
Taxable	£15,000		

All sums must be paid gross: it is no longer permissible to deduct tax on making payments.
The payer may elect to switch to the New Orders régime *below* if that would be to his advantage.

Payees
Tax is payable on up to the amount that the individual payee received in the 1988-89 tax year. No tax is payable on any surplus. A global amount may be rearranged to create tax free sums. For example, a wife may have had an order in 1988-89 of £10,000, and in favour of two children of £5,000 each: a global amount of £20,000. This can be rearranged by a consent order to 5p to the wife and £10,000 to each child, of which only £5,000 for each child will be taxable. Note that in such circumstances a child must be under 21 in order for the payer to receive relief.

The first £1,720 of maintenance received (whether for herself or for the benefit of her children) by a separated or former wife who has not remarried is tax free. This does not apply to sums paid direct to children, nor to sums paid to a mother for the benefit of non-marital children.

NEW ORDERS
Orders made on applications dated on or after 15 March 1988;
orders made after 30 June 1988 on applications made before 15 March 1988;
agreements made on or after 15 March 1988.

Payers
Relief is confined to a maximum of £1,720 and is given at 15%.
It is given only in respect of payments made (whether for herself or for the benefit of her children) to a separated or former wife who has not remarried. No relief is available for payments made direct to children, nor to a mother for the benefit of non-marital children.

Payees
No tax is payable on any sums received by way of maintenance.

ASSESSMENTS UNDER THE CHILD SUPPORT ACT 1991
Relief will be given in accordance with the above rules depending on whether or not the assessment is replacing an Old Order. The relief available to the payer will continue to be given even where the payments are collected and/or retained by the Child Support Agency.

NOTE This is a complicated topic. The basic rules are set out above. In a case involving any degree of complexity advisers should have careful regard to the relevant provisions of the Taxes Act 1988 and the Finance Act 1988.

Perpetual Calendar

The number opposite each of the years in the list below indicates which of the calendars on the following pages is the one for that year. Thus the number opposite 1999 is 6, so calendar 6 can be used as a 1999 calendar.

Leap years

Years divisible by four without remainder are leap years with 366 days instead of 365 (29 days in February instead of 28). However the last year of a century is not a leap year except when divisible by 400.

Easter Sunday

These dates apply unless there is a change to a fixed Easter.

1990	15 April	1997	30 March	2004	11 April
1991	31 March	1998	12 April	2005	27 March
1992	19 April	1999	4 April	2006	16 April
1993	11 April	2000	23 April	2007	8 April
1994	3 April	2001	15 April	2008	23 March
1995	16 April	2002	31 March	2009	12 April
1996	7 April	2003	20 April	2010	4 April

Year	Calendar	Year	Calendar	Year	Calendar	Year	Calendar	Year	Calendar	Year	Calendar
1901	3	1926	6	1951	2	1976	12	2001	2	2026	5
1902	4	1927	7	1952	10	1977	7	2002	3	2027	6
1903	5	1928	8	1953	5	1978	1	2003	4	2028	14
1904	13	1929	3	1954	6	1979	2	2004	12	2029	2
1905	1	1930	4	1955	7	1980	10	2005	7	2030	3
1906	2	1931	5	1956	8	1981	5	2006	1	2031	4
1907	3	1932	13	1957	3	1982	6	2007	2	2032	12
1908	11	1933	1	1958	4	1983	7	2008	10	2033	7
1909	6	1934	2	1959	5	1984	8	2009	5	2034	1
1910	7	1935	3	1960	13	1985	3	2010	6	2035	2
1911	1	1936	11	1961	1	1986	4	2011	7	2036	10
1912	9	1937	6	1962	2	1987	5	2012	8	2037	5
1913	4	1938	7	1963	3	1988	13	2013	3	2038	6
1914	5	1939	1	1964	11	1989	1	2014	4	2039	7
1915	6	1940	9	1965	6	1990	2	2015	5	2040	8
1916	14	1941	4	1966	7	1991	3	2016	13	2041	3
1917	2	1942	5	1967	1	1992	11	2017	1	2042	4
1918	3	1943	6	1968	9	1993	6	2018	2	2043	5
1919	4	1944	14	1969	4	1994	7	2019	3	2044	13
1920	12	1945	2	1970	5	1995	1	2020	11	2045	1
1921	7	1946	3	1971	6	1996	9	2021	6	2046	2
1922	1	1947	4	1972	14	1997	4	2022	7	2047	3
1923	2	1948	12	1973	2	1998	5	2023	1	2048	11
1924	10	1949	7	1974	3	1999	6	2024	9	2049	6
1925	5	1950	1	1975	4	2000	14	2025	4	2050	7

1

January
M	2	9	16	23	30
T	3	10	17	24	31
W	4	11	18	25	
T	5	12	19	26	
F	6	13	20	27	
S	7	14	21	28	
S	1	8	15	22	29

February
M	6	13	20	27
T	7	14	21	28
W	1	8	15	22
T	2	9	16	23
F	3	10	17	24
S	4	11	18	25
S	5	12	19	26

March
M	6	13	20	27
T	7	14	21	28
W	1	8	15	22	29
T	2	9	16	23	30
F	3	10	17	24	31
S	4	11	18	25
S	5	12	19	26

April
M	3	10	17	24
T	4	11	18	25
W	5	12	19	26
T	6	13	20	27
F	7	14	21	28
S	1	8	15	22	29
S	2	9	16	23	30

May
M	1	8	15	22	29
T	2	9	16	23	30
W	3	10	17	24	31
T	4	11	18	25
F	5	12	19	26
S	6	13	20	27
S	7	14	21	28

June
M	5	12	19	26
T	6	13	20	27
W	7	14	21	28
T	1	8	15	22	29
F	2	9	16	23	30
S	3	10	17	24
S	4	11	18	25

July
M	3	10	17	24	31
T	4	11	18	25
W	5	12	19	26
T	6	13	20	27
F	7	14	21	28
S	1	8	15	22	29
S	2	9	16	23	30

August
M	7	14	21	28
T	1	8	15	22	29
W	2	9	16	23	30
T	3	10	17	24	31
F	4	11	18	25
S	5	12	19	26
S	6	13	20	27

September
M	4	11	18	25
T	5	12	19	26
W	6	13	20	27
T	7	14	21	28
F	1	8	15	22	29
S	2	9	16	23	30
S	3	10	17	24

October
M	2	9	16	23	30
T	3	10	17	24	31
W	4	11	18	25
T	5	12	19	26
F	6	13	20	27
S	7	14	21	28
S	1	8	15	22	29

November
M	6	13	20	27
T	7	14	21	28
W	1	8	15	22	29
T	2	9	16	23	30
F	3	10	17	24
S	4	11	18	25
S	5	12	19	26

December
M	4	11	18	25
T	5	12	19	26
W	6	13	20	27
T	7	14	21	28
F	1	8	15	22	29
S	2	9	16	23	30
S	3	10	17	24	31

2

January
M	1	8	15	22	29
T	2	9	16	23	30
W	3	10	17	24	31
T	4	11	18	25
F	5	12	19	26
S	6	13	20	27
S	7	14	21	28

February
M	5	12	19	26
T	6	13	20	27
W	7	14	21	28
T	1	8	15	22
F	2	9	16	23
S	3	10	17	24
S	4	11	18	25

March
M	5	12	19	26
T	6	13	20	27
W	7	14	21	28
T	1	8	15	22	29
F	2	9	16	23	30
S	3	10	17	24	31
S	4	11	18	25

April
M	2	9	16	23	30
T	3	10	17	24
W	4	11	18	25
T	5	12	19	26
F	6	13	20	27
S	7	14	21	28
S	1	8	15	22	29

May
M	7	14	21	28
T	1	8	15	22	29
W	2	9	16	23	30
T	3	10	17	24	31
F	4	11	18	25
S	5	12	19	26
S	6	13	20	27

June
M	4	11	18	25
T	5	12	19	26
W	6	13	20	27
T	7	14	21	28
F	1	8	15	22	29
S	2	9	16	23	30
S	3	10	17	24

July
M	2	9	16	23	30
T	3	10	17	24	31
W	4	11	18	25
T	5	12	19	26
F	6	13	20	27
S	7	14	21	28
S	1	8	15	22	29

August
M	6	13	20	27
T	7	14	21	28
W	1	8	15	22	29
T	2	9	16	23	30
F	3	10	17	24	31
S	4	11	18	25
S	5	12	19	26

September
M	3	10	17	24
T	4	11	18	25
W	5	12	19	26
T	6	13	20	27
F	7	14	21	28
S	1	8	15	22	29
S	2	9	16	23	30

October
M	1	8	15	22	29
T	2	9	16	23	30
W	3	10	17	24	31
T	4	11	18	25
F	5	12	19	26
S	6	13	20	27
S	7	14	21	28

November
M	5	12	19	26
T	6	13	20	27
W	7	14	21	28
T	1	8	15	22	29
F	2	9	16	23	30
S	3	10	17	24
S	4	11	18	25

December
M	3	10	17	24	31
T	4	11	18	25
W	5	12	19	26
T	6	13	20	27
F	7	14	21	28
S	1	8	15	22	29
S	2	9	16	23	30

Perpetual Calendar

3

	January	February	March	April
M	7 14 21 28	4 11 18 25	4 11 18 25	1 8 15 22 29
T	1 8 15 22 29	5 12 19 26	5 12 19 26	2 9 16 23 30
W	2 9 16 23 30	6 13 20 27	6 13 20 27	3 10 17 24
T	3 10 17 24 31	7 14 21 28	7 14 21 28	4 11 18 25
F	4 11 18 25	1 8 15 22	1 8 15 22 29	5 12 19 26
S	5 12 19 26	2 9 16 23	2 9 16 23 30	6 13 20 27
S	6 13 20 27	3 10 17 24	3 10 17 24 31	7 14 21 28

	May	June	July	August
M	6 13 20 27	3 10 17 24	1 8 15 22 29	5 12 19 26
T	7 14 21 28	4 11 18 25	2 9 16 23 30	6 13 20 27
W	1 8 15 22 29	5 12 19 26	3 10 17 24 31	7 14 21 28
T	2 9 16 23 30	6 13 20 27	4 11 18 25	1 8 15 22 29
F	3 10 17 24 31	7 14 21 28	5 12 19 26	2 9 16 23 30
S	4 11 18 25	1 8 15 22 29	6 13 20 27	3 10 17 24 31
S	5 12 19 26	2 9 16 23 30	7 14 21 28	4 11 18 25

	September	October	November	December
M	2 9 16 23 30	7 14 21 28	4 11 18 25	2 9 16 23 30
T	3 10 17 24	1 8 15 22 29	5 12 19 26	3 10 17 24 31
W	4 11 18 25	2 9 16 23 30	6 13 20 27	4 11 18 25
T	5 12 19 26	3 10 17 24 31	7 14 21 28	5 12 19 26
F	6 13 20 27	4 11 18 25	1 8 15 22 29	6 13 20 27
S	7 14 21 28	5 12 19 26	2 9 16 23 30	7 14 21 28
S	1 8 15 22 29	6 13 20 27	3 10 17 24	1 8 15 22 29

4

	January	February	March	April
M	6 13 20 27	3 10 17 24	3 10 17 24 31	7 14 21 28
T	7 14 21 28	4 11 18 25	4 11 18 25	1 8 15 22 29
W	1 8 15 22 29	5 12 19 26	5 12 19 26	2 9 16 23 30
T	2 9 16 23 30	6 13 20 27	6 13 20 27	3 10 17 24
F	3 10 17 24 31	7 14 21 28	7 14 21 28	4 11 18 25
S	4 11 18 25	1 8 15 22	1 8 15 22 29	5 12 19 26
S	5 12 19 26	2 9 16 23	2 9 16 23 30	6 13 20 27

	May	June	July	August
M	5 12 19 26	2 9 16 23 30	7 14 21 28	4 11 18 25
T	6 13 20 27	3 10 17 24	1 8 15 22 29	5 12 19 26
W	7 14 21 28	4 11 18 25	2 9 16 23 30	6 13 20 27
T	1 8 15 22 29	5 12 19 26	3 10 17 24 31	7 14 21 28
F	2 9 16 23 30	6 13 20 27	4 11 18 25	1 8 15 22 29
S	3 10 17 24 31	7 14 21 28	5 12 19 26	2 9 16 23 30
S	4 11 18 25	1 8 15 22 29	6 13 20 27	3 10 17 24 31

	September	October	November	December
M	1 8 15 22 29	6 13 20 27	3 10 17 24	1 8 15 22 29
T	2 9 16 23 30	7 14 21 28	4 11 18 25	2 9 16 23 30
W	3 10 17 24	1 8 15 22 29	5 12 19 26	3 10 17 24 31
T	4 11 18 25	2 9 16 23 30	6 13 20 27	4 11 18 25
F	5 12 19 26	3 10 17 24 31	7 14 21 28	5 12 19 26
S	6 13 20 27	4 11 18 25	1 8 15 22 29	6 13 20 27
S	7 14 21 28	5 12 19 26	2 9 16 23 30	7 14 21 28

5

	January	February	March	April
M	5 12 19 26	2 9 16 23	2 9 16 23 30	6 13 20 27
T	6 13 20 27	3 10 17 24	3 10 17 24 31	7 14 21 28
W	7 14 21 28	4 11 18 25	4 11 18 25	1 8 15 22 29
T	1 8 15 22 29	5 12 19 26	5 12 19 26	2 9 16 23 30
F	2 9 16 23 30	6 13 20 27	6 13 20 27	3 10 17 24
S	3 10 17 24 31	7 14 21 28	7 14 21 28	4 11 18 25
S	4 11 18 25	1 8 15 22	1 8 15 22 29	5 12 19 26

	May	June	July	August
M	4 11 18 25	1 8 15 22 29	6 13 20 27	3 10 17 24 31
T	5 12 19 26	2 9 16 23 30	7 14 21 28	4 11 18 25
W	6 13 20 27	3 10 17 24	1 8 15 22 29	5 12 19 26
T	7 14 21 28	4 11 18 25	2 9 16 23 30	6 13 20 27
F	1 8 15 22 29	5 12 19 26	3 10 17 24 31	7 14 21 28
S	2 9 16 23 30	6 13 20 27	4 11 18 25	1 8 15 22 29
S	3 10 17 24 31	7 14 21 28	5 12 19 26	2 9 16 23 30

	September	October	November	December
M	7 14 21 28	5 12 19 26	2 9 16 23 30	7 14 21 28
T	1 8 15 22 29	6 13 20 27	3 10 17 24	1 8 15 22 29
W	2 9 16 23 30	7 14 21 28	4 11 18 25	2 9 16 23 30
T	3 10 17 24	1 8 15 22 29	5 12 19 26	3 10 17 24 31
F	4 11 18 25	2 9 16 23 30	6 13 20 27	4 11 18 25
S	5 12 19 26	3 10 17 24 31	7 14 21 28	5 12 19 26
S	6 13 20 27	4 11 18 25	1 8 15 22 29	6 13 20 27

6

	January	February	March	April
M	4 11 18 25	1 8 15 22	1 8 15 22 29	5 12 19 26
T	5 12 19 26	2 9 16 23	2 9 16 23 30	6 13 20 27
W	6 13 20 27	3 10 17 24	3 10 17 24 31	7 14 21 28
T	7 14 21 28	4 11 18 25	4 11 18 25	1 8 15 22 29
F	1 8 15 22 29	5 12 19 26	5 12 19 26	2 9 16 23 30
S	2 9 16 23 30	6 13 20 27	6 13 20 27	3 10 17 24
S	3 10 17 24 31	7 14 21 28	7 14 21 28	4 11 18 25

	May	June	July	August
M	3 10 17 24 31	7 14 21 28	5 12 19 26	2 9 16 23 30
T	4 11 18 25	1 8 15 22 29	6 13 20 27	3 10 17 24 31
W	5 12 19 26	2 9 16 23 30	7 14 21 28	4 11 18 25
T	6 13 20 27	3 10 17 24	1 8 15 22 29	5 12 19 26
F	7 14 21 28	4 11 18 25	2 9 16 23 30	6 13 20 27
S	1 8 15 22 29	5 12 19 26	3 10 17 24 31	7 14 21 28
S	2 9 16 23 30	6 13 20 27	4 11 18 25	1 8 15 22 29

	September	October	November	December
M	6 13 20 27	4 11 18 25	1 8 15 22 29	6 13 20 27
T	7 14 21 28	5 12 19 26	2 9 16 23 30	7 14 21 28
W	1 8 15 22 29	6 13 20 27	3 10 17 24	1 8 15 22 29
T	2 9 16 23 30	7 14 21 28	4 11 18 25	2 9 16 23 30
F	3 10 17 24	1 8 15 22 29	5 12 19 26	3 10 17 24 31
S	4 11 18 25	2 9 16 23 30	6 13 20 27	4 11 18 25
S	5 12 19 26	3 10 17 24 31	7 14 21 28	5 12 19 26

7

	January	February	March	April
M	3 10 17 24 31	7 14 21 28	7 14 21 28	4 11 18 25
T	4 11 18 25	1 8 15 22	1 8 15 22 29	5 12 19 26
W	5 12 19 26	2 9 16 23	2 9 16 23 30	6 13 20 27
T	6 13 20 27	3 10 17 24	3 10 17 24 31	7 14 21 28
F	7 14 21 28	4 11 18 25	4 11 18 25	1 8 15 22 29
S	1 8 15 22 29	5 12 19 26	5 12 19 26	2 9 16 23 30
S	2 9 16 23 30	6 13 20 27	6 13 20 27	3 10 17 24

	May	June	July	August
M	2 9 16 23 30	6 13 20 27	4 11 18 25	1 8 15 22 29
T	3 10 17 24 31	7 14 21 28	5 12 19 26	2 9 16 23 30
W	4 11 18 25	1 8 15 22 29	6 13 20 27	3 10 17 24 31
T	5 12 19 26	2 9 16 23 30	7 14 21 28	4 11 18 25
F	6 13 20 27	3 10 17 24	1 8 15 22 29	5 12 19 26
S	7 14 21 28	4 11 18 25	2 9 16 23 30	6 13 20 27
S	1 8 15 22 29	5 12 19 26	3 10 17 24 31	7 14 21 28

	September	October	November	December
M	5 12 19 26	3 10 17 24 31	7 14 21 28	5 12 19 26
T	6 13 20 27	4 11 18 25	1 8 15 22 29	6 13 20 27
W	7 14 21 28	5 12 19 26	2 9 16 23 30	7 14 21 28
T	1 8 15 22 29	6 13 20 27	3 10 17 24	1 8 15 22 29
F	2 9 16 23 30	7 14 21 28	4 11 18 25	2 9 16 23 30
S	3 10 17 24	1 8 15 22 29	5 12 19 26	3 10 17 24 31
S	4 11 18 25	2 9 16 23 30	6 13 20 27	4 11 18 25

8

	January	February	March	April
M	2 9 16 23 30	6 13 20 27	5 12 19 26	2 9 16 23 30
T	3 10 17 24 31	7 14 21 28	6 13 20 27	3 10 17 24
W	4 11 18 25	1 8 15 22 29	7 14 21 28	4 11 18 25
T	5 12 19 26	2 9 16 23	1 8 15 22 29	5 12 19 26
F	6 13 20 27	3 10 17 24	2 9 16 23 30	6 13 20 27
S	7 14 21 28	4 11 18 25	3 10 17 24 31	7 14 21 28
S	1 8 15 22 29	5 12 19 26	4 11 18 25	1 8 15 22 29

	May	June	July	August
M	7 14 21 28	4 11 18 25	2 9 16 23 30	6 13 20 27
T	1 8 15 22 29	5 12 19 26	3 10 17 24 31	7 14 21 28
W	2 9 16 23 30	6 13 20 27	4 11 18 25	1 8 15 22 29
T	3 10 17 24 31	7 14 21 28	5 12 19 26	2 9 16 23 30
F	4 11 18 25	1 8 15 22 29	6 13 20 27	3 10 17 24 31
S	5 12 19 26	2 9 16 23 30	7 14 21 28	4 11 18 25
S	6 13 20 27	3 10 17 24	1 8 15 22 29	5 12 19 26

	September	October	November	December
M	3 10 17 24	1 8 15 22 29	5 12 19 26	3 10 17 24 31
T	4 11 18 25	2 9 16 23 30	6 13 20 27	4 11 18 25
W	5 12 19 26	3 10 17 24 31	7 14 21 28	5 12 19 26
T	6 13 20 27	4 11 18 25	1 8 15 22 29	6 13 20 27
F	7 14 21 28	5 12 19 26	2 9 16 23 30	7 14 21 28
S	1 8 15 22 29	6 13 20 27	3 10 17 24	1 8 15 22 29
S	2 9 16 23 30	7 14 21 28	4 11 18 25	2 9 16 23 30

Perpetual Calendar

9

	January	February	March	April
M	1 8 15 22 29	5 12 19 26	4 11 18 25	1 8 15 22 29
T	2 9 16 23 30	6 13 20 27	5 12 19 26	2 9 16 23 30
W	3 10 17 24 31	7 14 21 28	6 13 20 27	3 10 17 24
T	4 11 18 25	1 8 15 22 29	7 14 21 28	4 11 18 25
F	5 12 19 26	2 9 16 23	1 8 15 22 29	5 12 19 26
S	6 13 20 27	3 10 17 24	2 9 16 23 30	6 13 20 27
S	7 14 21 28	4 11 18 25	3 10 17 24 31	7 14 21 28

	May	June	July	August
M	6 13 20 27	3 10 17 24	1 8 15 22 29	5 12 19 26
T	7 14 21 28	4 11 18 25	2 9 16 23 30	6 13 20 27
W	1 8 15 22 29	5 12 19 26	3 10 17 24 31	7 14 21 28
T	2 9 16 23 30	6 13 20 27	4 11 18 25	1 8 15 22 29
F	3 10 17 24 31	7 14 21 28	5 12 19 26	2 9 16 23 30
S	4 11 18 25	1 8 15 22 29	6 13 20 27	3 10 17 24 31
S	5 12 19 26	2 9 16 23 30	7 14 21 28	4 11 18 25

	September	October	November	December
M	2 9 16 23 30	7 14 21 28	4 11 18 25	2 9 16 23 30
T	3 10 17 24	1 8 15 22 29	5 12 19 26	3 10 17 24 31
W	4 11 18 25	2 9 16 23 30	6 13 20 27	4 11 18 25
T	5 12 19 26	3 10 17 24 31	7 14 21 28	5 12 19 26
F	6 13 20 27	4 11 18 25	1 8 15 22 29	6 13 20 27
S	7 14 21 28	5 12 19 26	2 9 16 23 30	7 14 21 28
S	1 8 15 22 29	6 13 20 27	3 10 17 24	1 8 15 22 29

10

	January	February	March	April
M	7 14 21 28	4 11 18 25	3 10 17 24 31	7 14 21 28
T	1 8 15 22 29	5 12 19 26	4 11 18 25	1 8 15 22 29
W	2 9 16 23 30	6 13 20 27	5 12 19 26	2 9 16 23 30
T	3 10 17 24 31	7 14 21 28	6 13 20 27	3 10 17 24
F	4 11 18 25	1 8 15 22 29	7 14 21 28	4 11 18 25
S	5 12 19 26	2 9 16 23	1 8 15 22 29	5 12 19 26
S	6 13 20 27	3 10 17 24	2 9 16 23 30	6 13 20 27

	May	June	July	August
M	5 12 19 26	2 9 16 23 30	7 14 21 28	4 11 18 25
T	6 13 20 27	3 10 17 24	1 8 15 22 29	5 12 19 26
W	7 14 21 28	4 11 18 25	2 9 16 23 30	6 13 20 27
T	1 8 15 22 29	5 12 19 26	3 10 17 24 31	7 14 21 28
F	2 9 16 23 30	6 13 20 27	4 11 18 25	1 8 15 22 29
S	3 10 17 24 31	7 14 21 28	5 12 19 26	2 9 16 23 30
S	4 11 18 25	1 8 15 22 29	6 13 20 27	3 10 17 24 31

	September	October	November	December
M	6 13 20 27		3 10 17 24	1 8 15 22 29
T	7 14 21 28	1 8 15 22 29	4 11 18 25	2 9 16 23 30
W	1 8 15 22 29	2 9 16 23 30	5 12 19 26	3 10 17 24 31
T	2 9 16 23 30	3 10 17 24 31	6 13 20 27	4 11 18 25
F	3 10 17 24	4 11 18 25	7 14 21 28	5 12 19 26
S	4 11 18 25	5 12 19 26	1 8 15 22 29	6 13 20 27
S	5 12 19 26	6 13 20 27	2 9 16 23 30	7 14 21 28

11

	January	February	March	April
M	6 13 20 27	3 10 17 24	2 9 16 23 30	6 13 20 27
T	7 14 21 28	4 11 18 25	3 10 17 24 31	7 14 21 28
W	1 8 15 22 29	5 12 19 26	4 11 18 25	1 8 15 22 29
T	2 9 16 23 30	6 13 20 27	5 12 19 26	2 9 16 23 30
F	3 10 17 24 31	7 14 21 28	6 13 20 27	3 10 17 24
S	4 11 18 25	1 8 15 22 29	7 14 21 28	4 11 18 25
S	5 12 19 26	2 9 16 23	1 8 15 22 29	5 12 19 26

	May	June	July	August
M	4 11 18 25	1 8 15 22 29	6 13 20 27	3 10 17 24 31
T	5 12 19 26	2 9 16 23 30	7 14 21 28	4 11 18 25
W	6 13 20 27	3 10 17 24	1 8 15 22 29	5 12 19 26
T	7 14 21 28	4 11 18 25	2 9 16 23 30	6 13 20 27
F	1 8 15 22 29	5 12 19 26	3 10 17 24 31	7 14 21 28
S	2 9 16 23 30	6 13 20 27	4 11 18 25	1 8 15 22 29
S	3 10 17 24 31	7 14 21 28	5 12 19 26	2 9 16 23 30

	September	October	November	December
M	7 14 21 28	5 12 19 26	2 9 16 23 30	7 14 21 28
T	1 8 15 22 29	6 13 20 27	3 10 17 24	1 8 15 22 29
W	2 9 16 23 30	7 14 21 28	4 11 18 25	2 9 16 23 30
T	3 10 17 24	1 8 15 22 29	5 12 19 26	3 10 17 24 31
F	4 11 18 25	2 9 16 23 30	6 13 20 27	4 11 18 25
S	5 12 19 26	3 10 17 24 31	7 14 21 28	5 12 19 26
S	6 13 20 27	4 11 18 25	1 8 15 22 29	6 13 20 27

12

	January	February	March	April
M	5 12 19 26	2 9 16 23	1 8 15 22 29	5 12 19 26
T	6 13 20 27	3 10 17 24	2 9 16 23 30	6 13 20 27
W	7 14 21 28	4 11 18 25	3 10 17 24 31	7 14 21 28
T	1 8 15 22 29	5 12 19 26	4 11 18 25	1 8 15 22 29
F	2 9 16 23 30	6 13 20 27	5 12 19 26	2 9 16 23 30
S	3 10 17 24 31	7 14 21 28	6 13 20 27	3 10 17 24
S	4 11 18 25	1 8 15 22 29	7 14 21 28	4 11 18 25

	May	June	July	August
M	3 10 17 24 31	7 14 21 28	5 12 19 26	2 9 16 23 30
T	4 11 18 25	1 8 15 22 29	6 13 20 27	3 10 17 24 31
W	5 12 19 26	2 9 16 23 30	7 14 21 28	4 11 18 25
T	6 13 20 27	3 10 17 24	1 8 15 22 29	5 12 19 26
F	7 14 21 28	4 11 18 25	2 9 16 23 30	6 13 20 27
S	1 8 15 22 29	5 12 19 26	3 10 17 24 31	7 14 21 28
S	2 9 16 23 30	6 13 20 27	4 11 18 25	1 8 15 22 29

	September	October	November	December
M	6 13 20 27	4 11 18 25	1 8 15 22 29	6 13 20 27
T	7 14 21 28	5 12 19 26	2 9 16 23 30	7 14 21 28
W	1 8 15 22 29	6 13 20 27	3 10 17 24	1 8 15 22 29
T	2 9 16 23 30	7 14 21 28	4 11 18 25	2 9 16 23 30
F	3 10 17 24	1 8 15 22 29	5 12 19 26	3 10 17 24 31
S	4 11 18 25	2 9 16 23 30	6 13 20 27	4 11 18 25
S	5 12 19 26	3 10 17 24 31	7 14 21 28	5 12 19 26

13

	January	February	March	April
M	4 11 18 25	1 8 15 22 29	7 14 21 28	4 11 18 25
T	5 12 19 26	2 9 16 23	1 8 15 22 29	5 12 19 26
W	6 13 20 27	3 10 17 24	2 9 16 23 30	6 13 20 27
T	7 14 21 28	4 11 18 25	3 10 17 24 31	7 14 21 28
F	1 8 15 22 29	5 12 19 26	4 11 18 25	1 8 15 22 29
S	2 9 16 23 30	6 13 20 27	5 12 19 26	2 9 16 23 30
S	3 10 17 24 31	7 14 21 28	6 13 20 27	3 10 17 24

	May	June	July	August
M	2 9 16 23 30	6 13 20 27	4 11 18 25	1 8 15 22 29
T	3 10 17 24 31	7 14 21 28	5 12 19 26	2 9 16 23 30
W	4 11 18 25	1 8 15 22 29	6 13 20 27	3 10 17 24 31
T	5 12 19 26	2 9 16 23 30	7 14 21* 28	4 11 18 25
F	6 13 20 27	3 10 17 24	1 8 15 22 29	5 12 19 26
S	7 14 21 28	4 11 18 25	2 9 16 23 30	6 13 20 27
S	1 8 15 22 29	5 12 19 26	3 10 17 24 31	7 14 21 28

	September	October	November	December
M	5 12 19 26	3 10 17 24 31	7 14 21 28	5 12 19 26
T	6 13 20 27	4 11 18 25	1 8 15 22 29	6 13 20 27
W	7 14 21 28	5 12 19 26	2 9 16 23 30	7 14 21 28
T	1 8 15 22 29	6 13 20 27	3 10 17 24	1 8 15 22 29
F	2 9 16 23 30	7 14 21 28	4 11 18 25	2 9 16 23 30
S	3 10 17 24	1 8 15 22 29	5 12 19 26	3 10 17 24 31
S	4 11 18 25	2 9 16 23 30	6 13 20 27	4 11 18 25

14

	January	February	March	April
M	3 10 17 24 31	7 14 21 28	6 13 20 27	3 10 17 24
T	4 11 18 25	1 8 15 22 29	7 14 21 28	4 11 18 25
W	5 12 19 26	2 9 16 23	1 8 15 22 29	5 12 19 26
T	6 13 20 27	3 10 17 24	2 9 16 23 30	6 13 20 27
F	7 14 21 28	4 11 18 25	3 10 17 24 31	7 14 21 28
S	1 8 15 22 29	5 12 19 26	4 11 18 25	1 8 15 22 29
S	2 9 16 23 30	6 13 20 27	5 12 19 26	2 9 16 23 30

	May	June	July	August
M	1 8 15 22 29	5 12 19 26	3 10 17 24 31	7 14 21 28
T	2 9 16 23 30	6 13 20 27	4 11 18 25	1 8 15 22 29
W	3 10 17 24 31	7 14 21 28	5 12 19 26	2 9 16 23 30
T	4 11 18 25	1 8 15 22 29	6 13 20 27	3 10 17 24 31
F	5 12 19 26	2 9 16 23 30	7 14 21 28	4 11 18 25
S	6 13 20 27	3 10 17 24	1 8 15 22 29	5 12 19 26
S	7 14 21 28	4 11 18 25	2 9 16 23 30	6 13 20 27

	September	October	November	December
M	4 11 18 25	2 9 16 23 30	6 13 20 27	4 11 18 25
T	5 12 19 26	3 10 17 24 31	7 14 21 28	5 12 19 26
W	6 13 20 27	4 11 18 25	1 8 15 22 29	6 13 20 27
T	7 14 21 28	5 12 19 26	2 9 16 23 30	7 14 21 28
F	1 8 15 22 29	6 13 20 27	3 10 17 24	1 8 15 22 29
S	2 9 16 23 30	7 14 21 28	4 11 18 25	2 9 16 23 30
S	3 10 17 24	1 8 15 22 29	5 12 19 26	3 10 17 24 31

Leading Cases

Adjournment of claims

Morris v Morris	(1977) 7 Fam Law 244, CA
Priest v Priest	(1980) FLR 189, CA
Milne v Milne	(1981) FLR 286, CA
Hardy v Hardy	(1981) FLR 321, CA
Davies v Davies	[1986] 1 FLR 497, CA
Roberts v Roberts	[1986] 2 All ER 483, [1986] 1 WLR 437, [1986] 2 FLR 152
Michael v Michael	[1986] 2 FLR 389, CA
Ranson v Ranson	[1988] 1 WLR 183, [1988] 1 FLR 292, CA
MT v MT (financial provision: lump sum)	[1992] 1 FLR 362

Agreements

Hyman v Hyman	[1929] AC 601, [1929] All ER Rep 245, HL
Backhouse v Backhouse	[1978] 1 All ER 1158, [1978] 1 WLR 243
Dean v Dean	[1978] Fam 161, [1978] 3 All ER 758, [1978] 3 WLR 288
Edgar v Edgar	[1980] 3 All ER 887, [1980] 1 WLR 1410, (1981) FLR 19, CA
Camm v Camm	(1983) FLR 577, CA
Simister v Simister (No. 2)	[1987] 1 FLR 194
Amey v Amey	[1992] 2 FLR 89
N v N	[1993] 2 FLR 868, CA
Pounds v Pounds	[1994] 1 WLR 1535, [1994] 4 All ER 777, [1994] 1 FLR 775, CA
Richardson v Richardson (No. 2)	[1994] 2 FLR 1051

Appealing out of time

Johnson v Johnson	(1980) FLR 331, CA
Warren v Warren	(1983) FLR 529, CA
Barder v Barder (Caluori intervening)	[1988] AC 20, [1987] 2 All ER 440, [1987] 2 WLR 1350, HL
Rooker v Rooker	[1988] 1 FLR 219, CA
Hope-Smith v Hope-Smith	[1989] 2 FLR 56, CA
Edmonds v Edmonds	[1990] 2 FLR 202, CA
Smith v Smith	[1992] Fam 69, [1991] 2 All ER 306, [1991] 3 WLR 646, CA
Thompson v Thompson	[1991] 2 FLR 530, CA
Wells v Wells	[1992] 2 FLR 66, CA
Chaudhuri v Chaudhuri	[1992] 2 FLR 73, CA
Rundle v Rundle	[1992] 2 FLR 80, CA
Barber v Barber	[1993] 1 FLR 476, CA
Re C (financial provision: leave to appeal)	[1993] 2 FLR 799
Crozier v Crozier	[1994] Fam 114, [1994] 2 All ER 362, [1994] 2 WLR 444
Cornick v Cornick	[1994] 2 FLR 530
Penrose v Penrose	[1994] 2 FLR 621, CA
Worlock v Worlock	[1994] 2 FLR 689, CA

Appeals

Ladd v Marshall	[1954] 3 All ER 745, [1954] 1 WLR 1489, CA
G (formerly P) v P (ancillary relief: appeal)	[1978] 1 All ER 1099, [1977] 1 WLR 1376, CA
Marsh v Marsh	[1993] 2 All ER 794, [1993] 1 WLR 744, [1993] 1 FLR 467, CA

Arrears

Fowler v Fowler	(1981) FLR 141, CA
Russell v Russell	[1986] 1 FLR 465, CA
Bernstein v O'Neill	[1989] 2 FLR 1

Avoidance of dispositions

Green v Green	[1981] 1 All ER 97, [1981] 1 WLR 391
K v K	(1983) FLR 31, CA
Kemmis v Kemmis	[1988] 1 WLR 1307, [1988] 2 FLR 223, CA
Sherry v Sherry	[1991] 1 FLR 307, CA

Leading Cases

Bankruptcy

Re Holliday (a bankrupt)	[1981] Ch 405, [1980] 3 All ER 385, CA
Davy-Chiesman v Davy-Chiesman	[1984] Fam 48, [1984] 1 All ER 321, [1984] 2 WLR 291, CA
Re Dennis (a bankrupt)	[1993] Ch 72, [1992] 3 All ER 436, [1992] 3 WLR 204
Re Flint (a bankrupt)	[1993] Ch 319, [1993] 2 WLR 537, [1993] 1 FLR 763
Re Kumar (a bankrupt)	[1993] 2 All ER 700, [1993] 1 WLR 224, [1993] 2 FLR 382
Woodley v Woodley (No.2)	[1993] 4 All ER 1010, [1994] 1 WLR 1167, [1993] 2 FLR 477, CA
Re Pavlou (a bankrupt)	[1993] 3 All ER 955, [1993] 1 WLR 1046, [1993] 2 FLR 751
F v F (divorce: insolvency: annulment of bankruptcy order)	[1994] 1 FLR 359
Chohan v Saggar	[1994] BCC 135, CA
Re Dent (a bankrupt)	[1994] 2 All ER 904, [1994] 1 WLR 956, [1994] 2 FLR 540, Div Ct

Banks

Barclays Bank plc v O'Brien	[1994] 1 AC 180, [1993] 4 All ER 417, [1993] 3 WLR 786, HL
CIBC Mortgages plc v Pitt	[1994] 1 AC 200, [1993] 4 All ER 433, [1993] 3 WLR 802, HL
Lloyds Bank plc v Waterhouse	[1993] 2 FLR 97, CA
Midland Bank v Massey	[1994] 2 FLR 342, CA
Midland Bank v Greene	[1994] 2 FLR 827

Children (capital provision)

Chamberlain v Chamberlain	[1974] 1 All ER 33, [1973] 1 WLR 1557, CA
Lilford (Lord) v Glyn	[1979] 1 All ER 441, [1979] 1 WLR 78, CA
Griffiths v Griffiths	[1984] Fam 70, [1984] 2 All ER 626, [1984] 3 WLR 165, CA
Kiely v Kiely	[1988] 1 FLR 248, CA
K v K	[1992] 2 All ER 727, [1992] 1 WLR 530, [1992] 2 FLR 220, CA
J v J (a minor: property transfer)	[1993] 2 FLR 56
A v A (minor: capital provision)	[1994] 1 FLR 657
T v S (financial provision for children)	[1994] 2 FLR 883

Children (non-marital, income provision)

Haroutunian v Jennings	(1980) FLR 62, Div Ct
Osborn v Sparks	(1982) FLR 90, Div Ct

Child Support Act

Crozier v Crozier	[1994] Fam 114, [1994] 2 All ER 362, [1994] 2 WLR 444
B v M (child support: revocation of order)	[1994] 1 FLR 342
B v McL (leave to appeal)	[1994] Fam Law 182
Re E (a minor) (child support: blood test)	[1994] 2 FLR 548, [1995] 1 FCR 245
Mawson v Mawson	[1994] 2 FLR 985
Smith v McInerney	[1994] 2 FLR 1077
Re C (Child Support Agency: disclosure)	[1995] 1 FLR 201, [1995] 1 FCR 202
B v Secretary of State for Social Security	(1995) Times 28 January

Clean break/termination

Hanlon v Hanlon	[1978] 2 All ER 889, [1978] 1 WLR 592, CA
Pearce v Pearce	(1980) FLR 261, CA
Morris v Morris	[1985] FLR 1176, CA
Seaton v Seaton	[1986] 2 FLR 398, CA
S v S	[1986] Fam 189, [1986] 3 All ER 566, [1986] 3 WLR 518; on appeal [1987] 2 All ER 312, [1987] 1 WLR 382n, CA
M v M	[1987] 2 FLR 1
Suter v Suter & Jones	[1987] Fam 111, [1987] 2 All ER 336, [1987] 3 WLR 9, CA

Leading Cases

Clean break/termination (Cont'd)

Whiting v Whiting	[1988] 2 All ER 275, [1988] 1 WLR 565, [1988] 2 FLR 189, CA
Barrett v Barrett	[1988] 2 FLR 516
C v C	[1989] 1 FLR 11
Hepburn v Hepburn	[1989] 1 FLR 373, CA
Waterman v Waterman	[1989] 1 FLR 380, CA
Fisher v Fisher	[1989] 1 FLR 423, CA
Clutton v Clutton	[1991] 1 All ER 340, [1991] 1 WLR 359, [1991] 1 FLR 242, CA
H v H	[1993] 2 FLR 35
Richardson v Richardson	[1993] 4 All ER 673, [1994] 1 WLR 186, [1994] 1 FLR 286
M v M	[1993] 2 FLR 723, CA
N v N (consent order: variation)	[1993] 2 FLR 868, CA
Richardson v Richardson (No. 2)	[1994] 2 FLR 1051

Companies

Potter v Potter	[1982] 3 All ER 321, [1982] 1 WLR 1255, (1983) FLR 331, CA
Smith v Smith	(1983) FLR 154, CA
Re Bird Precision Bellows	[1984] Ch 419, [1984] 3 All ER 444, [1984] 2 WLR 869
Nicholas v Nicholas	[1984] FLR 285, CA
Buckingham v Francis	[1986] 2 All ER 738
Bullock v Bullock	[1986] 1 FLR 372, CA
B v B	[1989] 1 FLR 119
P v P	[1989] 2 FLR 241
Evans v Evans	[1990] 2 All ER 147, [1990] 1 FLR 319
Poon v Poon	[1994] 2 FLR 857

Conduct

Sexual

Brett v Brett	[1969] 1 All ER 1007, [1969] 1 WLR 487, CA
Harnett v Harnett	[1973] Fam 156, [1973] 2 All ER 593, [1973] 3 WLR 1; affd [1974] 1 All ER 764, [1974] 1 WLR 219, CA
Cuzner v Underdown	[1974] 2 All ER 351, [1974] 1 WLR 641, CA
Bailey v Tolliday	(1983) FLR 542

Violence, etc

Jones v Jones	[1976] Fam 8, [1975] 2 All ER 12, [1975] 2 WLR 606, CA
M v M (financial provision: conduct)	(1982) FLR 83
Kyte v Kyte	[1988] Fam 145, [1987] 3 All ER 1041, [1987] 3 WLR 1114, CA
Evans v Evans	[1989] 1 FLR 351, CA
H v H (financial provision: conduct)	[1994] 2 FLR 801

Financial misconduct

Martin v Martin	[1976] Fam 335, [1976] 3 All ER 625, [1976] 3 WLR 580, CA
Primavera v Primavera	[1992] 1 FLR 16, CA

Misconduct of proceedings

B v B (real property: assessment of interests)	[1988] 2 FLR 490
T v T (interception of documents)	[1994] 2 FLR 1083

Other

Robinson v Robinson	(1981) FLR 1, CA
Robinson v Robinson	[1983] Fam 42, [1983] 1 All ER 391, [1983] 2 WLR 146, CA
Vasey v Vasey	[1985] FLR 596, CA
K v K (conduct)	[1990] 2 FLR 225
Whiston v Whiston	[1994] 2 FLR 906

Leading Cases

Costs

Inter partes

Calderbank v Calderbank	[1976] Fam 93, [1975] 3 All ER 333, [1975] 3 WLR 586, CA
Cutts v Head	[1984] Ch 290, [1984] 1 All ER 597, [1984] 2 WLR 349, CA
Moorish v Moorish	[1984] Fam Law 26, CA
Singer v Sharegin	[1984] FLR 114, CA
Atkinson v Atkinson	[1984] FLR 524, CA
Leadbeater v Leadbeater	[1985] FLR 789
Leary v Leary	[1987] 1 All ER 261, [1987] 1 WLR 72, [1987] 1 FLR 384, CA
S v S	[1989] FCR 570
E v E	[1990] 2 FLR 233
Gojkovic v Gojkovic (No.2)	[1992] Fam 40, [1992] 1 All ER 267, [1991] 3 WLR 621, CA *1991 2FLR 233*
In re Elgindata Ltd (No.2)	[1993] 1 All ER 232, [1992] 1 WLR 1207, CA
H v H	[1993] 2 FLR 35
Thompson v Thompson (costs)	[1993] 2 FLR 464, CA

Orders against legal advisers

Chrulew v Borm-Reid & Co	[1992] 1 All ER 953, [1992] 1 WLR 176
Ridehalgh v Horsefield	[1994] Ch 205, [1994] 3 All ER 848, [1994] 3 WLR 462, CA
C v C (wasted costs order)	[1994] 2 FLR 34
Sarra v Sarra	[1994] 2 FLR 880; sub nom S v S [1995] 1 FCR 185

Delay

Lombardi v Lombardi	[1973] 3 All ER 625, [1973] 1 WLR 1276, CA
Chaterjee v Chaterjee	[1976] Fam 199, [1976] 1 All ER 719, [1976] 2 WLR 397, CA
Chambers v Chambers	(1980) FLR 10
Fraser v Fraser	(1982) FLR 98, CA
D v W	(1984) 14 Fam Law 152
Twiname v Twiname	[1992] 1 FLR 29, CA

Division by one-third

Wachtel v Wachtel	[1973] Fam 72, [1973] 1 All ER 829, [1973] 2 WLR 366, CA
Sibley v Sibley	(1981) FLR 121
Furniss v Furniss	(1982) FLR 46, CA

Farms

P v P	[1978] 3 All ER 70, [1978] 1 WLR 483, CA
S v S	(1980) 10 Fam Law 240

Financial relief after overseas divorce

Holmes v Holmes	[1989] Fam 47, [1989] 3 All ER 786, [1989] 3 WLR 302, CA
Z v Z (foreign divorce: financial provision)	[1992] 2 FLR 291
M v M (financial provision after foreign divorce)	[1994] 1 FLR 399
Hewitson v Hewitson	[1995] 1 All ER 472, [1995] 1 FLR 241, CA

Inheritance (Provision for Family and Dependants) Act

Re Coventry, Coventry v Coventry	[1980] Ch 461, [1979] 3 All ER 815, [1979] 3 WLR 802, CA
Re Besterman (deceased)	[1984] Ch 458, [1984] 2 All ER 656, [1984] 3 WLR 280, CA
Bishop v Plumley	[1991] 1 All ER 236, [1991] 1 WLR 582, [1991] 1 FLR 121, CA
Moody v Stevenson	[1992] Ch 486, [1992] 2 All ER 524, [1992] 2 WLR 640, CA
Jessop v Jessop	[1992] 1 FLR 591, CA
Powell v Osbourne	[1993] 1 FLR 1001, CA
Davis v Davis	[1993] 1 FLR 54, CA
Re Jennings (deceased)	[1994] Ch 286, [1994] 3 All ER 27, [1994] 3 WLR 67, CA

Leading Cases

Injunctions in support of ancillary relief

Section 37 injunctions

Jordan v Jordan	(1965) Sol Jo 353
Smith v Smith	(1974) 4 Fam Law 80
Jackson v Jackson	(1979) 9 Fam Law 56, CA
Hamlin v Hamlin	[1986] Fam 11, [1985] 2 All ER 1037, [1985] 3 WLR 629, CA
Crittenden v Crittenden	[1990] 2 FLR 361, CA
Shipman v Shipman	[1991] 1 FLR 250

Mareva injunctions

Mareva Cia Naviera SA v International Bulkcarriers SA	[1980] 1 All ER 213, CA
Roche v Roche	(1981) 11 Fam Law 243, CA
PCW (Underwriting Agencies) Ltd v Dixon	[1983] 2 All ER 158 and 697
Law Society v Shanks	[1988] 1 FLR 504, CA
Lloyds Bowmaker Ltd v Britannia Arrow Holdings plc (Lavens, third party)	[1988] 3 All ER 178, [1988] 1 WLR 1337, CA
Brink's-MAT Ltd v Elcombe	[1988] 3 All ER 188, [1988] 1 WLR 1350, CA
Babanaft International Co SA v Bassatne	[1990] Ch 13, [1989] 1 All ER 433, [1989] 2 WLR 232, CA
Derby & Co Ltd v Weldon (No.1)	[1989] 1 All ER 469, [1989] 2 WLR 276, CA
Derby & Co Ltd v Weldon (No.2)	[1989] 1 All ER 1002, CA
Derby & Co Ltd v Weldon (No.6)	[1990] 3 All ER 263, [1990] 1 WLR 1189, CA
Shipman v Shipman	[1991] 1 FLR 250
Ghoth v Ghoth	[1992] 2 All ER 920, [1992] 2 FLR 300, CA

Anton Piller orders

Anton Piller KG v Manufacturing Processes Ltd	[1976] Ch 55, [1976] 1 All ER 779, CA
Cook Industries Incorporate v Galliher	[1979] Ch 439
Emanuel v Emanuel	[1982] 2 All ER 342, [1982] 1 WLR 669, (1982) FLR 319
Gates v Swift	[1982] RPC 339
Kepa v Kepa	(1983) FLR 515
Altertext Inc v Advanced Data Communications Ltd	[1985] 1 All ER 395, [1985] 1 WLR 457
Columbia Pictures v Robinson	[1986] FSR 367
Bhimji v Chatwani	[1991] 1 All ER 705, [1991] 1 WLR 989
Universal Thermosensors Ltd v Hibben	[1992] 3 All ER 257, [1992] 1 WLR 840

Writ ne exeat regno

Felton v Callis	[1969] 1 QB 200, [1968] 3 All ER 673
Al Nahkel Trading Ltd v Lowe	[1986] QB 235, [1986] 1 All ER 729
Bayer AG v Winter	[1986] 1 All ER 733, [1986] 1 WLR 497, CA
Thaha v Thaha	[1987] 2 FLR 142
Allied Arab Bank v Hajjar	[1988] QB 787, [1987] 3 All ER 789

Interim capital orders/orders for sale

Crosthwaite v Crosthwaite	[1989] 2 FLR 86, CA
Barry v Barry	[1992] Fam 140, [1992] 3 All ER 405, [1992] 2 WLR 799
Green v Green	[1993] 1 FLR 326

Joint names

Browne v Pritchard	[1975] 3 All ER 721, [1975] 1 WLR 1366, CA
Walsh v Corcoran	(1983) FLR 59, CA

Leading Cases

Legal aid
Effect on order
Collins v Collins   [1987] 1 FLR 226, CA
Scallon v Scallon   [1990] 1 FLR 194, CA

Incidence of charge
Till v Till   [1974] 1 QB 558, [1974] 1 All ER 1096, [1974] 2 WLR 447, CA
Hanlon v Law Society   [1981] AC 124, [1980] 2 All ER 199, [1980] 2 WLR 756, HL
Draskovic v Draskovic   (1981) 11 Fam Law 87
Manley v Law Society   [1981] 1 All ER 401, [1981] 1 WLR 335, CA
Van Hoorn v Law Society   [1985] QB 106, [1984] 3 All ER 136, [1984] 3 WLR 199
Curling v Law Society   [1985] 1 All ER 705, [1985] 1 WLR 470, [1985] FLR 831, CA
Stewart v Law Society   [1987] 1 FLR 223
Watkinson v Legal Aid Board   [1991] 2 All ER 953, [1991] 1 WLR 419, [1991] 2 FLR 26, CA
Parkes v Legal Aid Board   [1994] 2 FLR 850

Orders against Legal Aid Board
Nowotnik v Nowotnik   [1967] P 83, [1965] 3 All ER 167, [1965] 3 WLR 920, CA
Hanning v Maitland (No. 2)   [1970] 1 QB 580, [1970] 1 All ER 812, [1970] 2 WLR 151, CA
Povey v Povey   [1972] Fam 40, [1972] 3 All ER 612, [1971] 2 WLR 381, Div Ct
Middleton v Middleton   [1994] 1 FLR 557, CA
Keller v Keller   [1995] 1 FLR 259, CA

Length of marriage: cohabitation before
Campbell v Campbell   [1976] Fam 347, [1977] 1 All ER 1, [1976] 3 WLR 572
Kokosinski v Kokosinski   [1980] Fam 72, [1980] 1 All ER 1106, [1980] 3 WLR 55
Foley v Foley   [1981] Fam 160, [1981] 2 All ER 857, [1981] 3 WLR 284, CA

Length of marriage: short
S v S   [1977] Fam 127, [1977] 1 All ER 56, [1977] 3 WLR 775, CA
Churchill v Churchill   (1981) 11 Fam Law 179, CA
H v H   (1981) FLR 392
Robertson v Robertson   (1983) FLR 387
H (formerly W) v H   (1983) 13 Fam Law 180
Attar v Attar (No.2)   [1985] FLR 653
Hedges v Hedges   [1991] 1 FLR 196, CA

Lump sums
L v L (lump sum: interest)   [1994] 2 FLR 324
Masefield v Alexander (lump
  sum: extension of time)   [1995] 1 FLR 100, CA

Money, big
O'D v O'D   [1976] Fam 83, [1975] 2 All ER 993, [1975] 3 WLR 308, CA
Preston v Preston   [1982] Fam 17, [1982] 1 All ER 41, [1982] 3 WLR 619, CA
O'Neill v O'Neill   [1993] 2 FCR 297, CA
Re Besterman (deceased)   [1984] Ch 458, [1984] 2 All ER 656, [1984] 3 WLR 280, CA
Attar v Attar (No. 1)   [1985] FLR 649
S v S   [1986] Fam 189, [1986] 3 All ER 566, [1986] 3 WLR 518;
                                   on appeal [1987] 2 All ER 312, [1987] 1 WLR 382n, CA
Duxbury v Duxbury   [1992] Fam 62n, [1990] 2 All ER 77, [1991] 3 WLR 639, CA
Boylan v Boylan   [1988] 1 FLR 282
R v R (financial provision:
  reasonable needs)   [1994] 2 FLR 1044
Newton v Newton   [1990] 1 FLR 33, CA
Gojkovic v Gojkovic   [1992] Fam 40, [1990] 2 All ER 84, [1991] 3WLR 621, CA
B v B (financial provision:
  discovery)   [1990] 2 FLR 180
E v E   [1990] 2 FLR 233

Leading Cases

Money, big (Cont'd)

Vicary v Vicary	[1992] 2 FLR 271, CA
H v H (financial provision: capital allowance)	[1993] 2 FLR 335
H v H (clean break: non-disclosure: costs)	[1994] 2 FLR 309
Van G v Van G (finance: millionaire's defence)	[1995] 1 FLR 328

Money, small

Barnes v Barnes	[1972] 3 All ER 872, [1972] 1 WLR 1381, CA
Peacock v Peacock	[1984] 1 All ER 1069, [1984] 1 WLR 532, [1984] FLR 263
Freeman v Swatridge	[1984] FLR 762, CA
Ashley v Blackman	[1988] Fam 85, [1988] 3 WLR 222, [1988] 2 FLR 278
Delaney v Delaney	[1990] 2 FLR 457, CA

Negligence (by legal advisers)

Dutfield v Gilbert H Stevens & Sons	(1988) 18 Fam Law 473
White v Jones	[1993] 3 All ER 481, [1993] 3 WLR 730, CA
Griffiths v Dawson & Co	[1993] 2 FLR 315
Dickinson v Jones Alexander & Co	[1993] 2 FLR 521

Net effect

Furniss v Furniss	(1982) FLR 46, CA
Stockford v Stockford	(1982) FLR 58, CA
Slater v Slater & Another	(1982) FLR 364, CA
Titheradge v Titheradge	(1983) FLR 552, CA
Allen v Allen	[1986] 2 FLR 265, CA

Non-disclosure/discovery

J v J	[1955] P 215, [1955] 3 WLR 72, [1955] 2 All ER 617, CA
Weisz v Weisz	(1975) Times 16 December, CA
Robinson v Robinson	[1982] 2 All ER 699, [1982] 1 WLR 786, (1983) FLR 102
Desai v Desai	(1983) 13 Fam Law 46
Livesey v Jenkins	[1985] AC 424, [1985] 1 All ER 106, [1985] 2 WLR 47, HL
B-T v B-T	[1990] 2 FLR 1
E v E	[1990] 2 FLR 233
G v G	[1992] 1 FLR 40
Hildebrand v Hildebrand	[1992] 1 FLR 244
F v F (divorce: insolvency: annulment of bankruptcy order)	[1994] 1 FLR 359
H v H (financial relief: non-disclosure: costs)	[1994] 2 FLR 94
C v C (financial provision: non-disclosure)	[1994] 2 FLR 272
P v P (financial relief: non-disclosure)	[1994] 2 FLR 381

Non-parties, disclosure by

Morgan v Morgan	[1977] Fam 122, [1977] 2 All ER 515, [1977] 2 WLR 712
Wynne v Wynne & Jeffers	[1980] 3 All ER 659, [1981] 1 WLR 69, (1980) 10 Fam Law 241, CA
W v W (disclosure by third party)	(1981) FLR 291
Re T (divorce: interim maintenance: discovery)	[1990] 1 FLR 1
Frary v Frary	[1993] 2 FLR 696, CA

Leading Cases

Orders on property

Mesher v Mesher & Hall	[1980] 1 All ER 126n, CA
Martin v Martin	[1978] Fam 12, [1977] 3 All ER 762, [1977] 3 WLR 101, CA
Dunford v Dunford	[1980] 1 All ER 122, [1980] 1 WLR 5, CA
Harvey v Harvey	[1982] Fam 83, [1982] 1 All ER 693, [1982] 2 WLR 283, CA
Thompson v Thompson	[1986] Fam 38, [1985] 2 All ER 243, [1985] 3 WLR 17, CA
Mortimer v Mortimer-Griffin	[1986] 2 FLR 315, CA
Clutton v Clutton	[1991] 1 All ER 340, [1991] 1 WLR 359, [1991] 1 FLR 242, CA
Popat v Popat	[1991] 2 FLR 163, CA

Parity of assets

Daubney v Daubney	[1976] Fam 267, [1976] 2 All ER 453, [1976] 2 WLR 959, CA
Page v Page	(1981) FLR 198, CA
Schuller v Schuller	[1990] 2 FLR 193, CA

Pensions

Military

Priest v Priest	(1980) FLR 189, CA
Walker v Walker	[1983] Fam 68, [1983] 2 All ER 909, [1983] 3 WLR 421, CA
Roberts v Roberts	[1986] 2 All ER 483, [1986] 1 WLR 437, [1986] 2 FLR 152
Ranson v Ranson	[1988] 1 WLR 183, [1988] 1 FLR 292, CA
Happé v Happé	[1991] 4 All ER 527, [1990] 1 WLR 1282, [1990] 2 FLR 212, CA
Legrove v Legrove	[1994] 2 FLR 119, CA

Other

Edmonds v Edmonds	[1965] 1 All ER 379n, [1965] 1 WLR 58
Le Marchant v Le Marchant	[1977] 3 All ER 610, [1977] 1 WLR 559, CA
Richardson v Richardson	(1979) 9 Fam Law 86, CA
Hedges v Hedges	[1991] 1 FLR 196, CA
Jackson v Jackson	[1993] 2 FLR 848, CA
Brooks v Brooks	[1994] 4 All ER 1065, [1994] 3 WLR 1292, [1994] 2 FLR 10, CA

Property, beneficial interest in

Sole name

Pettitt v Pettitt	[1970] AC 777, [1969] 2 All ER 385, [1969] 2 WLR 966, HL
Gissing v Gissing	[1971] AC 886, [1970] 2 All ER 780, [1970] 3 WLR 255, HL
Grant v Edwards	[1986] Ch 638, [1986] 2 All ER 426, [1986] 3 WLR 114, CA
Lloyds Bank plc v Rosset	[1991] 1 AC 107, [1990] 1 All ER 1111, [1990] 2 WLR 867, HL
Risch v McFee	[1991] 1 FLR 105, CA
Stokes v Anderson	[1991] 1 FLR 391
Hammond v Mitchell	[1992] 2 All ER 109, [1991] 1 WLR 1127; sub nom H v M [1992] 1 FLR 229
Tinsley v Milligan	[1994] 1 AC 340, [1993] 3 All ER 65, [1993] 3 WLR 126, HL

Joint names

Bernard v Josephs	[1982] Ch 391, [1982] 3 All ER 162, [1982] 2 WLR 1052, CA
Goodman v Gallant	[1986] Fam 106, [1986] 1 All ER 311, [1986] 2 WLR 236, CA
Marsh v von Sternberg	[1986] 1 FLR 526
Springette v Defoe	[1992] 2 FLR 388, CA
Huntingford v Hobbs	[1993] 1 FLR 736, CA
Savill v Goodall	[1993] 1 FLR 755, CA
Abbey National plc v Moss	[1994] 1 FLR 307, CA

Remarriage and cohabitation

Prospects

Wachtel v Wachtel	[1973] Fam 72, [1973] 1 All ER 829, [1973] 2 WLR 366, CA
S v S	[1976] Fam 18n, [1975] 2 WLR 615n; sub nom Smith v Smith, [1975] 2 All ER 19n
Livesey v Jenkins	[1985] AC 424, [1985] 1 All ER 106, [1985] 2 WLR 47, HL

Leading Cases

Remarriage and cohabitation (Cont'd)
Actual remarriage

H v H	[1975] Fam 9, [1975] 1 All ER 367, [1975] 2 WLR 124
Stockford v Stockford	(1982) FLR 58, CA
Prow (formerly Brown) v Brown	(1983) FLR 352, CA
Camm v Camm	(1983) FLR 577, CA

Cohabitation

Blower v Blower	[1986] 1 FLR 292
Suter v Suter and Jones	[1987] Fam 111, [1987] 2 All ER 336, [1987] 3 WLR 9, CA
Atkinson v Atkinson	[1988] Fam 93, [1987] 3 All ER 849, [1988] 2 WLR 204, CA
R v R	[1988] 1 FLR 89, CA
Hepburn v Hepburn	[1989] 1 FLR 373, CA
Duxbury v Duxbury	[1992] Fam 62n, [1990] 2 All ER 77, [1991] 3 WLR 639, CA

Resources, extent of

Lombardi v Lombardi	[1973] 3 All ER 625, [1973] 1 WLR 1276, CA
Armstrong v Armstrong	(1974) 4 Fam Law 156, CA
Daubney v Daubney	[1976] Fam 267, [1976] 2 All ER 453, [1976] 2 WLR 959, CA
P v P (financial provision)	[1978] 3 All ER 70, [1978] 1 WLR 483, CA
Pearce v Pearce	(1980) FLR 261, CA
Schuller v Schuller	[1990] 2 FLR 193, CA
Wagstaff v Wagstaff	[1992] 1 All ER 275, [1992] 1 WLR 320, [1992] 1 FLR 333, CA

Second wife/cohabitee, means of

Roberts v Roberts	[1970] P 1, [1968] 3 All ER 479, [1968] 3 WLR 1181, Div Ct
Macey v Macey	(1982) FLR 7
Slater v Slater & Another	(1982) FLR 364, CA
Suter v Suter & Jones	[1987] Fam 111, [1987] 2 All ER 336, [1987] 3 WLR 9, CA
Atkinson v Atkinson	[1988] Fam 93, [1987] 3 All ER 849, [1988] 2 WLR 204, CA

Trusts

Howard v Howard	[1945] P 1, [1945] 1 All ER 91, CA
Re Londonderry's Settlement	[1965] Ch 918, [1964] 3 All ER 855, [1965] 2 WLR 229, CA
B v B	(1982) FLR 298, CA
Browne v Browne	[1989] 1 FLR 291, CA
E v E	[1990] 2 FLR 233

Variation of final orders

Carson v Carson	[1983] 1 All ER 478, [1983] 1 WLR 285, (1981) FLR 352, CA
Sandford v Sandford	[1986] 1 FLR 412, CA
Thompson v Thompson	[1986] Fam 38, [1985] 2 All ER 243, [1985] 3 WLR 17, CA
Dinch v Dinch	[1987] 1 All ER 818, [1987] 1 WLR 252, [1987] 2 FLR 162, HL
Peacock v Peacock	[1991] 1 FLR 324
Popat v Popat	[1991] 2 FLR 163, CA

Variation of periodical payments orders

Primavera v Primavera	[1992] 1 FLR 16, CA
Garner v Garner	[1992] 1 FLR 573, CA

Matrimonial Causes Act 1973

25. Matters to which court is to have regard in deciding how to exercise its powers under ss. 23, 24 and 24A.

(1) It shall be the duty of the court in deciding whether to exercise its powers under section 23, 24 or 24A above and, if so, in what manner, to have regard to all the circumstances of the case, first consideration being given to the welfare while a minor of any child of the family who has not attained the age of eighteen.

(2) As regards the exercise of the powers of the court under section 23 (1) (a), (b) or (c), 24 or 24A above in relation to a party to the marriage, the court shall in particular have regard to the following matters –

(a) the income, earning capacity, property and other financial resources which each of the parties to the marriage has or is likely to have in the forseeable future, including in the case of earning capacity any increase in that capacity which it would in the opinion of the court be reasonable to expect a party to the marriage to take steps to acquire;

(b) the financial needs, obligations and responsibilities which each of the parties to the marriage has or is likely to have in the foreseeable future;

(c) the standard of living enjoyed by the family before the breakdown of the marriage;

(d) the age of each party to the marriage and the duration of the marriage;

(e) any physical or mental disability of either of the parties to the marriage;

(f) the contributions which each of the parties has made or is likely in the foreseeable future to make to the welfare of the family, including any contribution by looking after the home or caring for the family;

(g) the conduct of each of the parties, if that conduct is such that it would in the opinion of the court be inequitable to disregard it;

(h) in the case of proceedings for divorce or nullity of marriage, the value to each of the parties to the marriage of any benefit (for example, a pension) which, by reason of the dissolution or annulment of the marriage, that party will lose the chance of acquiring.

(3) As regards the exercise of the powers of the court under section 23 (1) (d), (e) or (f), (2) or (4), 24 or 24A above in relation to a child of the family, the court shall in particular have regard to the following matters –

(a) the financial needs of the child;

(b) the income, earning capacity (if any), property and other financial resources of the child;

(c) any physical or mental disability of the child;

(d) the manner in which he was being and in which the parties to the marriage expected him to be educated or trained;

(e) the considerations mentioned in relation to the parties to the marriage in paragraphs (a), (b), (c) and (e) of subsection (2) above.

(4) As regards the exercise of the powers of the court under section 23 (1) (d), (e) or (f), (2) or (4), 24 or 24A above against a party to a marriage in favour of a child of the family who is not the child of that party, the court shall also have regard –

(a) to whether that party assumed any responsibility for the child's maintenance, and, if so, to the extent to which, and the basis upon which, that party assumed such responsibility and to the length of time for which that party discharged such responsibility;

(b) to whether in assuming and discharging such responsibility that party did so knowing that the child was not his or her own;

(c) to the liability of any other person to maintain the child.

25A. Exercise of court's powers in favour of party to marriage on decree of divorce or nullity of marriage.

(1) Where on or after the grant of a decree of divorce or nullity of marriage the court decides to exercise its powers under section 23 (1) (a), (b) or (c), 24 or 24A above in favour of a party to the marriage, it shall be the duty of the court to consider whether it would be appropriate so to exercise those powers that the financial obligations of each party towards the other will be terminated as soon after the grant of the decree as the court considers just and reasonable.

(2) Where the court decides in such a case to make a periodical payments or secured periodical payments order in favour of a party to the marriage, the court shall in particular consider whether it would be appropriate to require those payments to be made or secured only for such term as would in the opinion of the court be sufficient to enable the party in whose favour the order is made to adjust without undue hardship to the termination of his or her financial dependence on the other party.

(3) Where on or after the grant of a decree of divorce or nullity of marriage an application is made by a party to the marriage for a periodical payments or secured periodical payments order in his or her favour, then, if the court considers that no continuing obligation should be imposed on either party to make or secure periodical payments in favour of the other, the court may dismiss the application with a direction that the applicant shall not be entitled to make any further application in relation to that marriage for an order under section 23 (1) (a) or (b) above.

Matrimonial Causes Act 1973

31. Variation, discharge, etc. of certain orders for financial relief.

(1) Where the court has made an order to which this section applies, then, subject to the provisions of this section and of section 28 (1A) above, the court shall have power to vary or discharge the order or to suspend any provision thereof temporarily and to revive the operation of any provision so suspended.

(2) This section applies to the following orders, that is to say –

(a) any order for maintenance pending suit and any interim order for maintenance;

(b) any periodical payments order;

(c) any secured periodical payments order;

(d) any order made by virtue of section 23 (3) (c) or 27 (7) (b) above (provision for payment of a lump sum by instalments);

(e) any order for a settlement of property under section 24 (1) (b) or for a variation of settlement under section 24 (1) (c) or (d) above, being an order made on or after the grant of a decree of judicial separation;

(f) any order made under section 24A (1) above for the sale of property.

(2A) Where the court has made an order referred to in subsection (2) (a), (b) or (c) above, then subject to the provisions of this section, the court shall have power to remit the payment of any arrears due under the order or of any part thereof.

(3) The powers exercisable by the court under this section in relation to an order shall be exercisable also in relation to any instrument executed in pursuance of the order.

(4) The court shall not exercise the powers conferred by this section in relation to an order for a settlement under section 24 (1) (b) or for a variation of settlement under section 24 (1) (c) or (d) above except on an application made in proceedings –

(a) for the rescission of the decree of judicial separation by reference to which the order was made, or

(b) for the dissolution of the marriage in question.

(5) No property adjustment order shall be made on an application for the variation of a periodical payments or secured periodical payments order made (whether in favour of a party to a marriage or in favour of a child of the family) under section 23 above, and no order for the payment of a lump sum shall be made on an application for the variation of a periodical payments or secured periodical payments order in favour of a party to a marriage (whether made under section 23 or under section 27 above).

(6) Where the person liable to make payments under a secured periodical payments order has died, an application under this section relating to that order (and to any order made under section 24A (1) above which requires the proceeds of sale of property to be used for securing those payments) may be made by the person entitled to payments under the periodical payments order or by the personal representatives of the deceased person, but no such application shall, except with the permission of the court, be made after the end of the period of six months from the date on which representation in regard to the estate of that person is first taken out.

(7) In exercising the powers conferred by this section the court shall have regard to all the circumstances of the case, first consideration being given to the welfare while a minor of any child of the family who has not attained the age of eighteen, and the circumstances of the case shall include any change in any of the matters to which the court was required to have regard when making the order to which the application relates, and –

(a) in the case of a periodical payments or secured periodical payments order made on or after the grant of a decree of divorce or nullity of marriage, the court shall consider whether in all the circumstances and after having regard to any such change it would be appropriate to vary the order so that payments under the order are required to be made or secured only for such further period as will in the opinion of the court be sufficient to enable the party in whose favour the order was made to adjust without undue hardship to the termination of those payments;

(b) in a case where the party against whom the order was made has died, the circumstances of the case shall also include the changed circumstances resulting from his or her death.

(8) The personal representatives of a deceased person against whom a secured periodical payments order was made shall not be liable for having distributed any part of the estate of the deceased after the expiration of the period of six months referred to in subsection (6) above on the ground that they ought to have taken into account the possibility that the court might permit an application under this section to be made after that period by the person entitled to payments under the order; but this subsection shall not prejudice any power to recover any part of the estate so distributed arising by virtue of the making of an order in pursuance of this section.

(9) In considering for the purposes of subsection (6) above the question when representation was first taken out, a grant limited to settled land or to trust property shall be left out of account and a grant limited to real estate or to personal estate shall be left out of account unless a grant limited to the remainder of the estate has previously been made or is made at the same time.

(10) Where the court, in exercise of its powers under this section, decides to vary or discharge a periodical payments or secured periodical payments order, then, subject to section 28 (1) and (2) above, the court shall have power to direct that the variation or discharge shall not take effect until the expiration of such period as may be specified in the order.